EFFECTIVE MEDIA C
in 90 MINUTE

For a complete list of Management Books 2000 titles, visit our web-site on www.mb2000.com

Other titles in the 'in Ninety Minutes' series are:

25 Management Techniques in 90 Minutes
Active Learning in 90 Minutes
Become a Meeting Anarchist in 90 Minutes
Budgeting in 90 Minutes
Building a Website Using a CMS in 90 Minutes
Faster Promotion in 90 Minutes
Find That Job in 90 Minutes
Forget Debt in 90 Minutes
Funny Business in 90 Minutes
Getting More Visitors to Your Website in 90 Minutes
Networking in 90 Minutes
Payroll in 90 Minutes
Perfect CVs in 90 Minutes
Practical Negotiating in 90 Minutes
Strengths Coaching in 90 Minutes
Supply Chain in 90 Minutes
Telling People in 90 Minutes
Understand Accounts in 90 Minutes
Working Together in 90 Minutes

... other titles will be added

Submissions of possible titles for this series or for management books in general will be welcome. MB2000 are always keen to discuss possible new works that might be added to their extensive list of books for people who mean business.

EFFECTIVE MEDIA COVERAGE in 90 Minutes

Ted Lamb

First published in 2007 by Management Books 2000 Ltd
Forge House, Limes Road
Kemble, Cirencester
Gloucestershire, GL7 6AD, UK
Tel: 0044 (0) 1285 771441
Fax: 0044 (0) 1285 771055
E-mail: info@mb2000.com
Web: www.mb2000.com

Printed and bound in Great Britain by 4edge Ltd of Hockley, Essex – www.4edge.co.uk

British Library Cataloguing in Publication Data is available

ISBN13 9781852525323

Contents

1

YOU ARE IT!

Badly-presented copy after expert treatment by a sub-editor

The hands go up, the AGM has made its choice – you are Company Press Officer! You are the chosen one who will make the firm and its doings shine in the greater world that exists outside the boardroom walls.

An election is of course just one route to the role of presenting your company's news and information to the public through newspapers, journals and radio and TV. Other press officers are arbitrarily co-opted ('Here, Harry – or Harriet – you have a way with words, don't you?') or assigned the duties as part of another job. Some simply fall into the part, volunteering because nobody else seems interested.

This book is for you, and for another species that has also appeared in the modern world, encouraged by vastly improved communications and information exchange – the freelance press, public relations and publicity officer. This can make a nice little business for the adventurous few who have dipped their toes in the water on being asked to do the odd 'write-up'.

While what follows is designed primarily as an aid for appointed press officers, the points it makes apply equally to freelancers seeking to canvass business from a variety of sources, in particular from organisations which feel unable to justify hiring a full-time or part-time 'town crier'. In that frock-coated, tricorn-hatted gent bawling news of this and that on high streets up and down the country we see the forerunner of what has become the undoubted art of successfully presenting information to the public by *getting it accepted and published via newspapers and other journals or broadcast on radio or TV.*

A lot of the information in this book is dedicated to the business of writing what has come to be known as the 'press release' or 'handout'. But as we all know, press releases are not the only means of getting news and events and product information across to the general populace via the media – competitions for event tickets and 'free offers' for example are other routes, and these too are discussed later in the book. It should also be noted that I use the term 'press officer' to represent also publicity officers and public relations officers. There may be some variations in the duties implied by these different titles but the core duty of disseminating corporate information to the outside world remains the same.

Pity the organisation that does not take the opportunity to publicise itself, with the possible exception of the secret services (and even they have to come out of the closet from time to time). For almost all organisations, publicity and promotional efforts can offer huge benefits – and this holds true right across spectrum of PR activity, from representing a local football team to feeding the media for a corporate giant. Just what some of these benefits are will be discussed later, but consider for a moment how much a story which shows your organisation in a good light might help sales, for example, as well as recruitment, or by the same token how an entertaining game report might attract more supporters or new players for a football club. That could well save corporate money that might have had to be spent on advertising. Indeed, some press releases come close to advertising copy in their own right, but a caution should be added that overt advertising rarely finds its way past an alert editor – news, or more properly information, has to have a worth in its own right. It has to be something the reader or listener or viewer would like to know (in the editor's opinion!).

News and information, I can hear you say, isn't always good. True, but without somebody who can help to keep things positive and upbeat even in adversity, doom can easily be intensified.

Not a job to be taken lightly then, being a press officer.

No. And it is not a simple one either. Not if you want to be good at it. But in the same breath it is not overly hard. And it can be very rewarding, and great fun. Also, for some at least, it can be a great career.

Which comes to another good reason for this book...

Just as it is unwise for any organisation to ignore publicity, it is also unwise to send out what you (or your boss or company board) regard as news without making sure it will have a good chance of being used. After a lifetime in the media it is astonishing how many press and PR operatives, from those in major companies down to humble parish council news officers, are unaware of the needs of media they are trying to feed, let alone the best way to engage the attention of, say, the local evening or weekly newspaper.

Why, many press officers ask, does the local press ignore everything I tell them? Why is our important news never picked up by the national media while the lesser triumphs of rival organisations are given space?

There are of course good reasons. All of them are discussed in these pages, which point to the good practices that gain you and your colleagues (or your client) the valuable public recognition they deserve.

They range from properly defining your target media areas to presenting material in an acceptable form. They are easily learned and assimilated and they should lead to an immediate improvement in publicity output and a corresponding rise in interest in your organisation and its products and services. And if you are a freelancer, up will go your reputation together with, hopefully, your annual income.

The rest is up to you.

Smoke signals and tom-toms

In the old 'cowboys and indians' Hollywood films of the last century, the indians used smoke signals and drums to disseminate information – fulfilling the dual purpose of calling the tribe to pow-wow or war and alerting the cowboys to (usually) trouble. Spreading the word does not just apply to keeping the outside world informed of your organisation's activities. In many instances, particularly in larger companies, it is also part of the Press Officer's job to inform the whole workforce of management decisions, restructuring and the like. Often there is also an opportunity to present the rather more cosy aspects of corporate life, such as somebody's wedding or a birth, to the corporate body at large. It does wonders for internal relationships and displaying a caring side to management image. The medium for this can be as basic as a notice board or as thorough as a periodic newsletter or house magazine.

Often a newsy company website which takes the Press Officer's input serves the same dual role as puffs of smoke and throbbing tom-toms.

By applying the same lessons learned for effectively disseminating news to the media to presenting internal information and/or working with such a website, you can make great strides in your journalistic skills *and* fulfil your role 'in the round'. But let's not forget that what we are principally talking about here is 'selling' news to the outside world.

First things first

From the word go, for effective press communications you need the equipment to do the job (or ready access to it). There are also certain conditions you should argue strongly for from the outset to help you work at peak efficiency. The freelancer will of course have to supply his or her own equipment unless they contract to work in-house with a client.

A PC or Mac with internet connection

No press officer can be expected to effectively serve today's media without the means of creating and keeping a permanent record of information and the means of quickly submitting it to its target. Many press officers need to travel and work in different locations, and in these cases they will need a portable modern laptop. Broadband connection is almost an essential now because of the slow speed and unreliability of dial-up services. Wireless enablement is additionally useful. While a lot of the media do their work with Apple Macs because of their design capabilities, they recognise that the rest of the world mostly uses PCs, and they are all geared to taking transmissions in Word. However, you should obviously avoid little-known word-processing programmes or operating systems which might be incompatible with the system(s) on which they will be received.

Should you work at home either as a freelancer or because you are volunteering your services for a club for example, or because the company wants an out-of-hours service from you, help with computer expenses and even capital costs should be sought.

Telephone

If you use your home phone or mobile on behalf of a company (or client), explain to them what you are spending on business calls. Be prepared to log calls made on behalf of the firm/organisation. Seek recompense for these costs as well as for paper, envelopes, postage, etc. Explore the income tax implications of a home office set-up with your accountant or the company's tax expert. The costs of heating and light as well as office space are often an allowable expense you can claim back.

Car use

If you are employed come to some arrangement over motoring expenses made on behalf of the organisation you represent. Be careful you are not infringing any motor insurance conditions by using the vehicle for work.

Representation at high level

Argue for attending your organisation's (or client's) major meetings and policy briefings even if this means pledging you will not disclose material discussed to the media without permission. Argue also for direct access to key players without tedious and time wasting memo exchanges and appointments – you might well need to talk to them in a hurry.

In addition you will want:

- A personalised company email address and dedicated phone number (if possible).
- Inclusion (with contact details) of your name and position on the company letterheads.
- Inclusion (with contact details) on the company website, *and* space or a page or more on this site for news (you might also need to ask for skilled help to upload it).
- A digital camera (and the ability to use it, download and transmit material) is increasingly useful to the modern press officer, company-employed as well as freelancer.

Now go to it – you have roughly 85 minutes left!

2

YOUR ROLE AND MOTIVATION

A short word about the special way you have to look at things taking place in the company or organisation you represent when you stand in the shoes of a press officer and you first think about sending out material for media consumption.

While you may share the ethos, outlook and aims of your employer, you are in the rather special position of a middleman – important to recognise, this, because it is where an awful lot of media contributors fall down. And rather than looking at things from the corporate point of view – which is by and large, 'I want this information more widely known in the outside world; see to it' – instead you have to regard everything in terms of its value to the media 'target' which will be considering it in a completely different light, that of 'newsworthiness'.

In time, taking this viewpoint becomes second nature, but at the outset it helps to run a very critical eye over your intended output and judge it as if you have nothing at all to do with your organisation but are instead a reader (or listener/viewer) seeking interest in a news page or aired TV or radio news bulletin.

Consider the following example. The managing director of your organisation wishes to kick off the annual report and accounts with a summary of his views on the state of the world. Towards the end of his report will come the far more newsworthy fact that the firm is about to take over another company.

In the corporate climate the MD probably gets everything he asks for and if he wants his views to come first in a handout that is how it shall be. The boss has spoken. Sadly for him, his judge is not in his pay, even if you are – the judge is a hard-bitten news editor or copytaster who will be asking himself questions like how many people (i.e. readers, listeners, viewers) will be interested in the contents of the handout in question, and further, how many lives this particular item might affect. And the result in this instance will be that the takeover is very interesting indeed, because it could lead to more jobs and other improvements in the local economy, whereas the MD's philosophising, worthy though it may be, is about as interesting to the average media consumer as yesterday's congealed leftover chips.

Why then put out material 'the wrong way round', with genuine points of interest buried where they may even be overlooked by the recipient?

From time to time it may be necessary to point out to your colleagues and bosses the fact that you are 'selling' news rather than just being the mouthpiece through which they wish everything to be channelled. While your heart is 100 per cent behind what the company is doing and the way it is doing it, putting things 'your' way is of paramount importance because of the simple fact that you know what will and what will not appeal to your media target(s).

I could even suggest that you might let company bigwigs try things their way from time to time and judge the results for themselves – but that would be entirely unprofessional!

And keeping to the analogy above, at the same time as dissuading the MD from boring the pants off everyone, why not ask yourself some of the questions that may be going through that news editor's head – with a little digging you might discover other facts to send out with your story, like how the intended takeover is affecting the company's share prices, and whether or not Personnel (now often known as the lengthier but in some eyes more impressive Human Resources department) is considering taking on more hands to cope with increased business.

Now you are starting to think like a professional. It *is* possible to serve both masters. Let's face it, you *have* to serve them both!

Past this hurdle there's a real chance to shine and make a very welcome contribution to your organisation:

- You can paint a picture of it as a fair minded, fair dealing, fair trading, go-ahead, modern thinking, employee-friendly, equal opportunity, customer-friendly, environment-friendly, consumer aware, community-involved, highly respected company (delete whichever is inappropriate and if none apply, quit!).

- You can help to raise the company or organisation's name/standing/profile locally and often nationally as well, keeping it always in the public eye with the judicious use of well-crafted handouts which take into account the considerations mentioned above.
- You can help to increase sales or in the case of sport/entertainments, attendances. You can in effect create a lot of 'free' advertising for the firm in areas like sales and recruitment.
- You can help to ease the organisation's way through setbacks as well as trumpeting its successes and victories.

To do this you need one simple motivation: to seek every opportunity no matter how small to give the company a 'name check'.

You may not always be recognised for your contribution to corporate success, because you are after all an 'invisible' asset for the most part. But do take the opportunity from time to time to point out that such-and-such could be a direct result of the handout you distributed last week. And if nobody then seems to give you any credit, at least you can pat yourself on the back when you know you are doing a great job.

3

DO IT NOW, DO IT CLEARLY AND CONCISELY

A couple more brief but important initial notes. First, the world of information is fast-moving. Strike while the iron is hot!

Never, never sit on news, no matter how wise a cautionary delay might seem, especially if it's 'big' or involves some kind of calamity (more about how to handle disasters later in the book). Tongues will wag, believe me. They always do. And somebody else will come along and dig the story out to present it in their own way, rather than yours, to the public. Consider the implications of that last sentence, especially the words 'in their own way'. This might not be in the same light that you would picture it in if you composed it. Worse, it could be hostile...

If you have a real humdinger of a story, and I'm thinking of things like a major takeover, collapse of shares, enormous profits, likely closure, a doubling of the workforce, the signing of a top-league player, the defection of half the team to your rival, the discovery of oil under the car park or all manner of things involving triumph or disaster, pick up the phone and call your contacts in the news organisations that are likely to do you the most good even while you are composing the story in your head. If it's big enough, good enough, they will create space and wait on your words.

In this case (and many others) it helps to be aware of the deadlines of your media targets, which are obviously not the same for an evening paper with several editions though the morning/afternoon as they are for a weekly paper or a national morning newspaper (I will deal later with the subject of manipulating deadlines to your advantage).

Many a newsroom wall bears the motto:

DO IT NOW.

It's a good one to adopt. And like everyone in a newsroom you have to be dynamic, do the job, move on...

Brevity

Often the handout that creates the most annoyance – and comes in for the roughest treatment even to the point of being discarded out of sheer bloody-mindedness – is the one that is too long. The gift of crisp and concise writing is not bestowed on everyone and it takes some time to learn this skill if you do not have it. In newsrooms young recruits (as well as many contributing press officers) are often the worst culprits, having learned the maxim 'it is better to have too much than too little'. It is very easy to let a word processor run away with you, easier than a typewriter I would dare to say. I remember one youngster seeking feedback from a chief sub editor on what he thought of one of his stories being fixed with a sardonic eye. 'Very wordy,' said the ancient (other newsroom inhabitants starting to snigger at this point), adding quickly: 'Oh, sorry, slip of the tongue ... I meant, very worthy, of course.'

Worse than having some of these faults themselves, press officers can sometimes find themselves pushed around a bit by company bigwigs (yes, it's *them* again) who want such and such included in a handout – usually some self-aggrandising statement to show they are doing their job. As I have suggested above, it is up to you to 'retrain' some of your superiors in the realities of 'selling' news and information. Councils on all levels can be the worst offenders here, also police press offices, and I sometimes shudder for the people who have to produce good work under these difficult circumstances. You can sometimes almost see the chief constable breathing down some unfortunate's neck.

Only in the heavyweight serious national newspapers will you find lengthy reports which go over the fine details point by point and draw from a wide variety of sources for background, colour and comment, and the finished article will certainly not look at all like an overlong press handout full of spurious detail and quotes. That's not only what the nationals do best but it is *their* job to undertake this 'in depth' treatment for the most part, rather than yours.

You can but deliver the facts, and draw some detail and comment from those around you. You could perhaps add a few facts from accessible sources like the current state of your shares in the stock market, but you may well not have the research resources necessary to treat material with this sort of thoroughness. Even if you did you would probably not have the time, as a one-man band rather than a newsroom full of experts and extras, to compose it. Nor indeed would most of your recipients below the heavyweight level thank you for it. Most of the media inhabits a world where six or seven paragraphs is the average length of a story, 250 words or thereabouts is page-lead length and 300 or more is getting into the realm where the average reader would find attention slipping – unless it's a well crafted feature piece which is an altogether different animal.

Thus the sub editor raises his pencil (or more likely his finger hovers over the delete button) when he reads the likes of

> Managing director John Cabot said: 'My grandfather Cornelius arrived in this country in 1929 with a farthing and a piece of string and went on to create this magnificent company through sheer guts and hard work while at the same time holding down jobs as an errand boy and a boot polisher. By 1930 at the time of great hardship he was employing two men and a boy and turning out yards of this black stuff, by now a trusted product in every household in the land. In April 1931...

and so on and so on, line after line, right down to

> ...and I feel sure he would be proud to see today that we have carried on where he left off and would be proud of the position we maintain as leading black stuff maker in Britain.

Out it goes, and instead is written:

> Managing Director John Cabot said his grandfather Cornelius Cabot, a poor immigrant and founder of the firm in 1929, would have been proud of the company's achievements.

Write your facts and comment, and if anything else pops up or is forced upon you look at it critically and ask yourself 'who gives a damn?'

If it doesn't pass this test leave it out. Go down a couple of spaces and write 'end'. Now send your handout off.

4

GROUND RULES

The golden rule

Forgive me for initially going over ground that more experienced press and public relations folk will already know well. It takes but a few of those precious minutes and you never know, even if you are a pro there may be a nugget or two of advice that you have overlooked or forgotten.

All you really need for this job is wits, a bit of storytelling ability, attention to accuracy (particularly where facts and figures and representing exactly what people say are concerned), and a sense of responsibility. That puts it within the capabilities of nearly everyone.

And it helps to like people.

Fulfil most of these needs and you are well on your way, but keep 'responsibility' especially in mind always. It's your golden rule. Why? Because this is the big element you need in the two-way traffic of disseminating news and information. Remember you are as responsible to your information target as much as you are to its source, the organisation that you represent.

Misrepresent your organisation, and you are clearly in trouble with those around you; misinform the media, deliberately or otherwise, and you break trust with your target. Of course mistakes can and do happen, and in some cases they can be put right, but deliberately or carelessly broken trust – either way – is fatal in the long run. And if you are mistrusted as an informant any future contribution you make to the media, no matter how newsworthy it may seem, will have to be questioned and perhaps rejected simply because the risk of using what may be more dodgy material from you is too great. Worse for you, news of this would quickly get around. The media may loom large in the public eye but it is actually a very small and fluid world where everyone pretty much knows everyone else.

Being honest can and does occasionally put the press officer in the position of having to make a stand, to say 'no' to the managing director who asks you to put about a downright lie (which is not the same, I might add, as being economical with the truth, though the distinction is a fine one). Fortunately this is rare, but the trust thing is a lesson best learned early which is why I have started with it. Your reliability is paramount to getting your voice heard. All other ground rules are secondary to this.

Be aware of your target's needs

We can move quickly on to defining media target areas and looking at how they handle incoming information. Having a good picture of what happens to the information you send out helps you to see ways of improving your output or perhaps pitching it to a new outlet for the first time (much more about this later in this book).

First some generalisations about the media as a whole.

Most people would be amazed how many hard-copy (typed or printed) and email press releases are unceremoniously dumped on a regular day-to-day basis by newspapers, magazines, and radio and TV stations. There is a good reason for the demise of each and every one of these discarded items. Most of all they show that whoever sent them in with the hope that they would be given newsprint space or airtime has not given much thought to how well they might be received (let alone how many trees might needlessly have been chopped to make the paper they are written on, or how much email ether they have clogged up).

The old newsroom name for the front-line man or woman who, like Caesar in the amphitheatre, gives the thumbs up or down to contributions arriving in any form, is a 'copytaster', a filtering role that is often combined with that of news editor. From here selected meatier articles go through the features editor, sporting pieces through the sports editor, and other items like finance, property, travel and so on through the relevant front-liners for the area concerned (depending on the payroll size of the organisation). A bit beside the point, but to help set the scene, on one free newspaper I currently freelance for, the editor fulfils all these roles with one assistant, while on bigger enterprises 'The Editor' is titular, representing the paper or the organisation in the wider world and rarely dirtying hands with nitty-gritty work. An army of minions covers the incumbent's back. But the copytaster rules supreme no matter what other tasks they undertake.

'Taster' is a good word. In olden times a 'taster' was employed by kings, queens and other bigwigs to take a nibble of their meals or a sip of wine to test if any poisoner had been at work, but the copy-taster's role is a little more refined in that he or she has to trawl for anything, and I mean anything, which has a nugget of newsworthiness buried within it. Such nuggets are rarely missed by the trained eye, for if you let one slip by you a rival is quite likely to pick it up instead. Close scrutiny and appraisal of contributions are watchwords.

So what goes into the bin?

- Items that are wildly off-target for the consumption of the reader/listener/viewer in terms of the journal or programme's subject matter.
- Items that have no relevance to the geographical 'patch' covered by the journal or programme.
- In general (though not always) items which seek overtly to advertise goods, services or upcoming events – particularly so if the recipient medium carries paid-for advertising. Often details of events like, say, an upcoming festival, will make the news slots because these are things an audience likes to know about – however the commercial details, such as where to obtain tickets and how much these will cost, is properly in the domain of advertising and it should not be surprising if they are omitted. Expect a call from an advertising rep if you send out this sort of material! Do not bother to remonstrate with the editor arguing that omitted details should be reinstated. The standard answer to this (with varying degrees of politeness) is,

'sorry, pal, but if I let yours go through every other bugger will want the same treatment'.

- Personal opinions which have no real currency beyond the bar or the boardroom, such as the managing director's annual rallying speech to the troops (unless it includes details of job creation or losses, significant financial or product changes – but the wise press officer should be alert for this).
- Gossip and hearsay are obviously no-go areas (and can be legally risky – more on this later) even though journalists are often called paid gossips.
- Some (admittedly occasional) material so badly written, messily or confusingly laid out and poorly presented that nobody has time to sort it out, especially working against the clock, before its news value has expired.
- Material that arrives bang on deadline, or too close to work on for an edition, especially in the case of weekly newspapers where rivals, be they dailies, evenings, nationals or other weeklies with later deadlines, will have 'done the thing to death' by the time the next edition comes round. Take heed of later notes on deadlines.

That's all? Pretty much. Yet the duff stuff comes in like a snowstorm compared with usable information. A lot of people are not doing their homework properly. A lot of people are being lazy, some would say, using a scatter-gun approach in the hope somebody, somewhere, will pick up their outpourings.

And is the rest that survives news?

Er, not exactly. In the words of one newspaper magnate, 'news is what people don't want you to know – all the rest is advertising.' There's some truth in that. Read your papers and magazines a little more critically, listen to the radio and TV reports a little more carefully, and you'll see what he meant.

For want of a better word what often passes for news is information – or to be more precise, usable information. Once this usable information has been separated from the dross the copy-taster/editor breaks it down into two further piles (let's be clear at this stage that radio and TV presenters work with written material just as newspapers and magazines do, and aired items have an allotted time span just as print items have to be sub-edited to fit an allotted space):

- **Material that can go straight to the sub-editors**
  A wild dream for any copy-taster unless the material has come from a 'pro' (which we will all try to be, won't we?) who has got it right. The sub-editors make the contribution fit the space (or time slot), check it for house 'style' (again, more about this later in the book) and write an appropriate headline. Copy 'ordered' from a press officer, that is sent in by agreement, may well fit this category, also prearranged and expected sports reports, etc.
- **Material that needs further treatment**
  This can vary from making a story out of a single highlighted fact (perhaps with further inquiries by a reporter) to a gentler rewrite which, in the copy-taster's opinion, will better present the facts. Sometimes material from the pile immediately above may also go into this pile because, although facts and presentation are fine, rival journals/stations will be looking at exactly the same duplicated information (unless it has been sent on an 'exclusive' basis) and if it does not have further treatment everyone will print/disseminate the same information word for word. Nobody wants to look as if they have been too lazy to write their own stories!

Keep it in mind also that (your) contributed material often only supplies half a story. In contentious stories this is particularly true. A complaint about council refuse services, for example, is unbalanced without somebody seeking the other side of the story, probably a quote from a council official explaining the difficulties they are facing, or apologising or otherwise.

Make sure leading characters in your organisation know what you are writing

Diplomacy can be an essential ingredient of representing any organisation or individual to the media. It is often not enough for a press officer to simply pull nuggets out of the managing director's annual speech to the nation. The great man's or the great lady's ego may well need to be massaged before you take such action. You may have to gently point out that if the whole speech is sent in to a paper or broadcasting station it will be savaged for its usable bits alone anyway, so the information might as well go out properly arranged for its news value in the first place. This does not mean of course that the (regrettably) redundant words do not have great value for the workforce, shareholders and so on, or that they have not been beautifully and skilfully selected, honed and crafted into a truly wonderful piece of oratory. (Soft soap? Of course!)

Watch your own back. Don't put out material that hasn't been officially approved unless you are a truly trusted representative of the organisation who has proved they can reliably work alone without checks (or unless you are the boss!). Seek agreement and note somewhere that you have gone through the motions of getting things officially checked. Weigh and assess whatever criticisms and advice you are given. And if you are the boss, ask yourself if you shouldn't let someone else read your craftwork before you send it out. Having something scanned with fresh eyes is valuable. They may spot glaring mistakes you have overlooked. Nobody's perfect. Not even you!

Around 75 minutes left, and counting!

5

THE NITTY-GRITTY

Assessing targets – the interest boundaries

Let's start by making clear once again that we are talking in the main about spreading information outside our organisation (or the client's organisation, if you are a freelancer) rather than the more 'cosy' house news. House news does of course become part of the role of many a press officer, particularly in large organisations where the management wants to spread the message to the workforce on matters of policy.

Here we are talking about interfacing with the outside world. It is often far from cosy, and the people who dwell in it are certainly not as unquestioning as a workforce that often has to take what it is given.

The sort of information you intend putting out depends of course on the type of organisation you represent – an obvious statement, I know. But you should always start out with the assumption that you want your outside coverage to be as wide as possible (it is after all what a lot of this book is about) and there will naturally be boundaries to the range of media, whether print or broadcast, who find 'your thing' at all interesting. Perhaps, though, 'boundaries' is a little too harsh, too definite – in many instances it will be a blurry line, sometimes quite a wide grey border.

Sometimes, though, the interest drop-off line can *seem* pretty sudden!

A local county league team's match report for example is of interest to the local weekly newspaper, and also the local evening if there is one. A reasonable amount of space may be allocated to it. The match may well also warrant a couple of seconds air time on a local radio station. But that could well be the limit of its range so far as media interest is concerned. If you are the team press officer in charge of match reports your job is done.

By the time the ante is upped to the regional morning newspaper, perhaps only a line will be spared for your result and league position. And unless anything startling happened at the event, such as the goalkeeper being struck by lightning, the regional television channels will not be at all interested either.

As to the national newspapers, radio stations and television channels … well, by and large, your match without a striking feature like an incinerated goalkeeper will mean absolutely nothing. You might as well have fallen off the edge of the world.

But wait just a second before you draw that line – didn't I say the drop-off might *seem* sudden. Doesn't that lead you to think there may be other scenarios?

Okay, the lightning thing doesn't happen every day, but plenty of other things do – perhaps your striker had to scoot off after scoring the first goal because his wife was rushed to hospital for the birth of his first child. Perhaps a freak tornado meant the match had to be abandoned. Perhaps ... well, a million such scenarios can probably be conjured up. My favourite (because I was actually there with the freelance journalist who reported it) occurred when a rabbit ran across the Peterborough dog track just after the 8.20 race had started. Off went the field after the rabbit, the hare forgotten. Race abandoned, long search for dogs. Scenarios like this make good copy for the nationals. Does it matter in the light of what we are talking about it? Well, had the track's then press officer reported it rather than my friend, he might have gained honour for the upsurge in interest in the dog track taken by the public – subsequent meetings saw much improved gates. The story also got into several magazines, which opens up a whole new 'market'. By the way, my friend did quite well financially out of the exercise!

Every press officer should start, however, by looking for the most appropriate targets for their reports, where interest is highest and the most print space or airtime might be expected. But you should always stay alert to the possibilities thrown up by exceptional circumstances.

Your 'main users' should in time become so familiar that things like phone numbers and email addresses, also the names of editors or news editors, come readily to mind.

Let's start by looking at 'actual users', 'possible users' and 'outside chances/other possibilities'.

As a little exercise, write down a 'desired user' list for the places you most obviously would like to run your information, and list also 'possible users', and 'outside chances/other possibilities'. Don't bother with names and numbers at this stage.

Some imaginary examples of 'desired users' are given below for six types of organisation which might be expected to have a press officer or at least someone tasked with representation to the media: Ambledown Women's Institute; Blighton Rangers, a county league football team in mid-table; Blighton Folk Museum and Gallery; Blighton Town Council; Blighton Soap, a growing Stock Exchange-listed company; and Barton Gas and Electricity, a listed public utility company. (Blighton is a fictitious market town, medium-sized, in fictitious Bartonshire – Barton being the county town and centre of local government. Ambledown is a village near Blighton, some say almost a suburb of the town these days!)

Now the media. With a few variations, the local press and broadcast make-up across the country is broadly similar to the one following. In our imaginary setting here is a local weekly paid-for paper, the Blighton Advertiser, which although based in Blighton actually serves quite a wide area (circulation 10,000 or so) as well as a weekly 'free' (Blighton Packet) which is stuck through letterboxes and has a proven distribution figure of 40,000 – vastly more than the 'paid-for' even though it serves virtually the same area. The 'free' strives to be competitive in news terms with the paid-for but has one big disadvantage in this respect – the space available week to week for news is governed entirely by the amount of advertising carried in each edition and sometimes there is very little space indeed. Because the considerable cost of distribution is borne by advertising revenue there is also very little money available to keep a full time journalist – many free papers are one-man-bands or even staffed by part-time freelancers. The paid-for on the other hand has a couple of reporters, a photographer and an editor who has the dual role of sub-editor. In competition with both these two is the Barton Evening News, published six days a week, which is part of a large national newspaper group. It 'editionalises' for the Blighton area – i.e. it loads some of its main news pages, if possible the front page, with Blighton-interest stories as well as carrying Barton and county news. It actually has a reporter based in Blighton, and of course an advertising office selling space and canvassing small-ads (classified advertisements). Its circulation within the Blighton area is however fairly small – 4,000 or so – but in its total circulation figure of only 35,000 this does actually represent more than 10 per cent of sales. Most daily evening newspapers today have falling circulations. There are a number of reasons, not least competition from other sources, such as 'instant' TV news at the flick of a button. Time was when each new edition was eagerly waited for to get the latest racing results!

In addition Barton has a commercial radio station and is also covered by roving regional BBC radio and television reporters.

The other major player in the localised scene is a regional daily (morning) newspaper, The Daily Westerner, which like the Barton Evening News is owned by a major media group. It is published in an adjacent county.

There are some smaller publications in this Blighton-centric model – there are three parish magazines, one in the town, and in nearby Ambledown village an enterprising soul has started a monthly gossip sheet, leaving a pile in the doctor's surgery for people to pick up. Oh, and there's a county magazine too, Bartonshire Life, largely concerned with property – expensive property! – and lifestyles.

Outside the cosy domestic world of the local media lies everything else – national daily and weekend newspapers, specialist papers like the Financial Times and Sporting Life, the BBC and other radio and television companies, magazines catering for thousands of different interests, newsletters, websites, blogs...

Ambledown W.I.

A lively little group that has an interesting speaker to each of its meetings along with the usual Jam and Jerusalem business – not forgetting the flower arrangement prize and the raffle draw. The treasurer used to also be press officer but this year there's a dedicated officer holding the post: Hilda Ronson. A notorious gossip, Hilda will bend your ear with every juicy bit of local scandal, real or imagined, although in her capacity as W.I. press officer she has been told (wisely) to keep strictly to the proceedings of meetings. She has found that the local gossip sheet publishes everything she writes about the W.I. without changing a single word. She is delighted about this and is thinking of contributing something more meaty to them off her own bat. If they take her up on this they had better beware – 'litigation' is becoming quite a familiar word!

When she took over the job, Hilda found she was expected to contribute regular pieces to the Ambledown parish magazine, the Blighton Advertiser, and also to the Barton Evening News for their Blighton edition.

Of these the parish magazine, like the gossip sheet, used almost all of her very full reports; the Blighton Advertiser used somewhat less, tediously to her mind cutting it to the same four paragraphs of the reports from other W.I.s; and the Barton Evening News often reduced her reports to little more than a paragraph – regular, nonetheless.

She had been told it was a 'waste of time' sending reports to the free paper, the Blighton Packet, but she had nevertheless (to her credit) ignored this and once or twice bits of material had been used – particularly a piece about a woman who was a specialist collector of historic knickers who would be coming to a future meeting. Because of the vast coverage in the 'free' the meeting was particularly well attended...

Enthusiastically, after this event, Hilda spread her wings and sent her reports to the Daily Westerner and called the regional broadcasters to ask if they wouldn't like to run a W.I. column. Alas, from the Westerner she heard nothing (though she did notice they ran a feature about her knickers lady, scarcely mentioning that she gave talks to W.I.s), while the newsrooms of the broadcasters said politely they regretted they had no airspace for reporting W.I. meetings.

There are a couple of points to take note of here: Firstly, it should be realised that Hilda writes but one report after each meeting and sends duplicates to all her users and prospective users. Should she take the trouble to 'tailor' each piece for its recipients (and of course if you are doing this you have to let the recipient know it is not just a duplicate) she would have more control over what is used. With a little more thought she could also spot the potential of the knickers story and make more of a pitch with it to the media outside her 'usual suspects'.

What then of Hilda's best customers?

Actual (desired) users:

1 **The Blighton Advertiser**
Why top, when they cut and sometimes rewrite her contributions? Answer: It has guaranteed dedicated media space in a place where it is seen by the most people.

2 **The Barton Evening News**
For the same reasons as above, even if contributions come in for rough treatment.

3 **The parish magazine**
Mainly because it is a regular and enduring institution.

4 **The gossip sheet**
Although copies are regularly available, for example at the local surgery waiting room, quirky little publications of this kind come and go but rarely last. People prefer the well-thumbed newsstand magazines in doctors' or dentists' waiting rooms, even if they haven't been changed since the turn of the millennium.

That's it? Practically, yes.

Exceptions? Hilda and those like her should always expect the unexpected and be prepared make the most of it. If everyone is driven out of the village hall by a swarm of bees, or if the Prime Minister's wife makes an unexpected visit and wins the raffle, it's a story with far wider appeal.

Blighton Rangers

The 'Rockets' as they are sometimes known have a strong local following on and off the field, with plenty of enthusiastic fans supporting home and away games and as many if not more following the team's fortunes in the local press. Their press officer is also the club secretary.

The Advertiser takes a regular match report often specifying the number of words needed. (N.B. Never, never send fewer words than the required amount – space to accommodate the report will already be set aside and it is always better to send too much – which can be cut – than too little.) The same sort of 'order' comes from the Barton Evening News for league matches, but the free newspaper is most of the time unable to use anything, although it sometimes makes exceptions for end-of-season play-offs and the like. There is a good reason for this – to run a dedicated sports results service you have to have dedicated space, and as mentioned above this is a luxury not available to a free newspaper where space is sometimes a feast but more often a famine.

When both the Advertiser and the Evening News ask for reports of the same match the team press officer does her best to 'tweak' the words so that they look different from each other, a refinement much appreciated by the two editorial departments because it saves them the work of doing this themselves.

On a wider front the Daily Westerner and local radio and TV stations sometimes ask for reports or a telephone call for a mini interview after the match. More often they are eager to hear final scorelines to keep league tables up to date. Informing the league secretary of the final score is also often the press officer's duty.

There's a wider field to serve than that, however. At least one national weekend paper occasionally asks for results ahead of the tables supplied through the league secretary. The Rockets fan club have their own website and notice board to which the press officer contributes. There are also soccer magazines and fanzines, print or on-line, which find some 'local' material interesting.

The parish magazine is rarely published more than once a month and is not interested in match reports. The gossip sheet is similarly uninterested, though they do go on a bit from time to time about people not cleaning up their dog poo on the recreation ground (but the press officer should monitor sources like this – perhaps there's a story in the dog poo menace for the 'real' papers, maybe even a chance to stir up a campaign).

Actual users

1 **Local radio** and **TV**, calls to **national papers** (usually result only), plus **The Barton Evening News** (as it is a daily, reports come out in the Monday issue a good two days ahead of the Advertiser). The criterion here is time. Serve the neediest first and never let 'em down.

2 **The Blighton Advertiser**. An important report which reaches by far the largest part of the fan base.

3 **Magazines** and **websites**.

Exceptions? We have already gone over some of the unexpected things that can happen at sporting events so there is no need to repeat this, other than to say, 'stay alert'!

Blighton Folk Museum and Gallery

This is much more than a museum, being partly commercial besides serving local history interests in a free display section. It takes touring exhibitions, some of which are ticketed events, as well as showing the work of local artists. It has an outdoor area which puts on displays of local crafts, in season, such as cider-making and charcoal burning, trying to run at least one commercial event a month (except in winter) with 'specials' appealing to families on spring and summer bank holiday weekends. It also caters for school parties and runs a small cafe and souvenir shop.

By far the biggest need it has from the local media is advertising. It does not have a huge budget and buying space is expensive. However, putting up good pre-event publicity along the lines of 'what a treat we have in store for you this weekend' can sometimes 'buy' free space in the form of a news feature. Overall publicity is well served if a local paper or broadcaster sums up how the crowds enjoyed themselves – these often make good picture features for newspapers, and TV stations include footage in weekend roundups and the like.

The museum's owners undertake their own publicity, putting out regular pre-event press handouts and keeping personally in touch with all their media contacts, aware how valuable even a small mention can be.

They have learned not to expect to see all the details they send out in their handouts: although they invariably include details of opening times, ticket prices and concessions, for example, these are often replaced in the media with wording like *'full details from the Museum'*. From a newspaper's point of view, giving such details is free advertising, and this is particularly true of the 'free' paper which relies entirely on advertising revenue. Also, if a paper does this for one firm it has an apparent duty to do it for everyone if it is to appear even-handed. Instead, the museum's owners have learned the best way to make the most of publicity is to run an advert in the same edition. However having said that, no newspaper will promise to run *any* contributed material whatsoever in case something more newsworthy comes along to take its place (e.g. 'drop the dead donkey') let alone run it beside an advertisement. The exception is something known as an 'advertising feature', labelled as such, where an advertiser and perhaps some support advertisers actually pay for the editorial space as well as the advert(s). Other tricks of the trade to 'buy' free editorial space are running competitions and offering free entry (or samples of goods) to winners or first-comers.

Main users

1. **The Blighton Packet**, the free paper with far and away the largest local circulation. The criterion here is getting event details and images of people having fun in front of as many people as possible.

2. **The Blighton Advertiser**, **Barton Evening News**, **The Daily Westerner**, and all **local radio** and **TV** stations

giving 'diary' events. It is occasionally worth sending each a different version of the handout, particularly if there is something special coming up, but the most likely scenario is that the information will appear in a much abbreviated form as a diary or 'what's on' item. Useful nonetheless.

3 **Bartonshire Life**. The magazine is worth contacting for a possible feature if something special is coming up, like willow-weaving (surprisingly popular) or hedge-laying.

4 **Specialist magazines** for particular subjects the museum may be displaying, such as canal-ware (boating magazines) or cider and beer making (Camra) or railway memorabilia, or ... the list is endless. Nevertheless it's 'free' publicity again, even if it only ends up in the events diary.

5 **National newspapers** and **websites** running events diaries. Outline details only need be sent.

Blighton Town Council

The Town Council and its officers come in for a lot of stick from time to time but do their best with limited resources. Often they are blamed for decisions taken a few local government tiers up, at district level or at county level in Shire Hall. Time and again it has been proved to them that it is best to do everything in a spirit of openness, transparency – and time and again intrigue crops up, and conspiracy theories flourish – yes, politics can be a dirty business, especially where overall control is marginal and an election is looming.

With only the same powers as a parish council yet with what seems a much wider remit, the town cannot afford a dedicated press officer but rests the responsibility on the shoulders of the town clerk.

Under his duty to let everyone know what is going on, the clerk sends out notices and minutes of all its meetings, and the decisions taken, to the local media as far as Barton, which is county level, but no further. He does not feel obliged to let the rest of the world look in on the town and nor should he. Neither does he feel obliged to explain anything in particular detail because all decisions are democratically voted upon and it's all in the minutes. If a paper or anyone else wants a story they can write one using this information. Nevertheless, if asked to comment on anything, the clerk will oblige, if only because his position is senior enough to allow him to have a public voice. Matters are varied, from arranging the Christmas lights, to helping create a skate park for local youth, and the clerk or the mayor will also pop along to ribbon-cutting opening ceremonies and switch-ons.

In circumstances where it is essential to place matter in the public gaze (sometimes a legal requirement) the clerk will often buy advertising space. Other than that, he simply needs to make sure he keeps his media contacts up to date, and sends them the meetings minutes and sundry notices (which incidentally are available to all at the town hall).

Main users:

1= **Blighton Advertiser**, **Blighton Packet**, **Barton Evening News** and **Radio Barton**.

2 **The Daily Westerner**

No other interest as a rule, but not from negativity – just well defined boundaries. Nevertheless there's a flavour of inertia…

Blighton Soap

This lovely little company grew up out of a hippy kitchen industry in the 1970s and it now employs 175 people producing quality floral scented soaps using organic materials – much sought after in posh shops as far away as London. It has recently gone public and is listed on the Stock Exchange. The firm is still growing, and facing up to an increasingly tough commercial world is not easy for its founders, who now have to represent shareholders too. A year ago (and shortly after listing) it was decided to hire a professional PR/press officer, Alison Key, who was attracted by an advertisement placed in a trade magazine. Her previous job, after a grounding in journalism with a local weekly paper, involved helping a businessman promote a small steam railway for train enthusiasts. This is her first product-based job and she has the added task of producing a monthly staff newsletter with the aim of keeping all levels of the organisation in touch with company policy and ethos. The share price is rising steadily, but there are rumours of takeover in the air...

As a pro Alison knows how to present product news in a form acceptable to news editors without it coming over as overt advertising (see how this is done in a later chapter).

She is privy to all management moves and is currently responding to wide national media interest in the takeover rumours. Nevertheless she is keen to keep the local news editors happy with material of interest to the community in which the company's workers live. As well as product and employment news she 'digs out' human interest stories involving personnel for the local papers as well as for her house newsletter and a lively notice board – a packer who is trekking across the Gobi Desert to raise funds for a local hospice, a woman who does Punch and Judy shows for weekend fetes, and so on. She has an eye for the pictorial prospects of items like this too, and often her picture suggestions are followed up by the press. For personnel stories, however, like the appointment of a new company accountant, she takes and supplies digital portraits of the people concerned.

Main users

1 (currently)	A lot of the **national newspapers** as well as **TV news**. The **financial papers** are particularly interested. Alison is aware that this is a critical period in the company's development and is anxious to get everything right – her releases are double-checked with management, and she takes special pains to avoid ambiguities and slips which could ultimately affect the share price and even the whole takeover.
2	All the **local media**, usually with human interest material, with Alison casting her net as wide as the Daily Westerner and regional TV and radio.
3	A big tranche of national bookstall **homekeeping magazines** (product news).

4 **Trade magazines** concerned with the sale of household goods (product news, some human interest stories).

Barton Gas and Electricity

Before the flotation of a number of public utility companies, this was simply Barton Gas; in its new guise it has become quite a big reseller of gas and electricity in a highly competitive market. Press and PR Officer Tony Williams has grown up with the company, working up from the floor since he joined as an office boy. He knows a lot of the local media people personally and also knows a story when he sees one – whether it's good news, like a refund for x-number of customers, or bad (more often, alas), like another price hike. He also knows some of the national financial journalists and often only has to drop a word or two in the right place, and his phone will be buzzing with newshounds after the story. He is available for TV and radio interviews and comes over as articulate but guarded. He still distributes press releases giving out company news, but self-limits his remit and does not deal in human-interest stories about company employees. The press releases are carefully checked at board level (he is not always invited to meetings) and if he thinks they sometimes appear over-corrected and dull he says nothing about this to the bosses. There is a company notice board but other than posting new rules and the like for staff he has little to do with it. Sometimes cuttings about the company appear on the board – indeed, it is a common complaint among the staff that they read about company changes in the newspapers or hear about it on television before anyone in the firm tells them anything at all.

Actual users

Tony Williams has a list of all **local and 'relevant' national media** to which he sends each and every company press release. Everybody gets the same release. Occasionally, if requested by the board to get national coverage urgently (sharply rising natural gas prices was the most recent of these occasions) he telephones people like the BBC's current energy expert. Once this story is 'broken' everyone else picks it up. He sees no point in casting the net any wider to, say, magazines or newsy websites.

Different priorities

Doesn't the above illustrate how different organisations have different priorities when it comes to disseminating information? You can judge the emphasis-shift in each and every one of them, and you can also see that some of the practitioners have shortcomings...

I'll leave you to judge which are the worse culprits for the moment, but I will make the comment that everyone can refresh their attitude to their work, and the rewards are often remarkable – even if they are just the satisfaction of doing a good job.

But don't leave this subject without turning the whole thing inside out. In the examples above we have taken a predominantly local perspective looking out towards national coverage. But, if you are working for a big national or international company, what about a national perspective looking down towards local coverage? Should you send out material to appeal to those 'little' weekly publications mentioned above – after all, an audience of 40,000 plus offered by the free newspaper is not to be sniffed at.

You bet you should! More about this too later on in the book.

Analysis

If you have followed my suggestion above and have written a list of the targets you would like to use your contributions, take a good long look at it, think of what your organisation does and makes or provides, and just let your imagination roam over the whole of the media smorgasbord, from parish magazines, through websites and up to the lofty heights of national television. At some point in your career, whatever organisation you represent, big or small, I can virtually guarantee you will come across something that will suit each and every one of these outlets – just like everyone being guaranteed their two minutes of fame. Be alert when these opportunities come!

A word about freelancing

Much, much more about this later, but for the present it is sufficient to say that all the roles used as illustrations above could form all or part of the client base of a very active freelance press and publicity officer – together with little bits of 'one off' work, say promoting a locally-based pop-group's tour or publicising a visiting pianist's concert, to add variety to the mix. The work of the freelance PR or press officer is not the same as that of the freelance journalist, although these careers can be – and often are – successfully combined.

6

KEEPING IN CONTACT

Find contacts, list them

Okay, so we have to start with a contacts list. With just a little bit of work we can make it a useful list, and with a bit more work still we can make it really, really, really useful...

Everyone in this trade needs a contacts book. Now I like computers, and they are pretty handy things when it comes to compiling lists of anything you care to mention, including contacts.

Trouble is, the contacts book is so valuable that losing it – or rather losing a computer file through viruses, negligence, carelessness, shifting files around when really too tired to do so, or a disastrous systems crash – can be like a stab to the heart. A contacts book built up over a number of years can be irreplaceable. Truly, I believe, committing contact details to paper is best. Best of all (theoretically at least) is a card index, with alphabetical tabs, so that new information can be added easily because you can write a lot on an ordinary index card, and new entries are similarly easy. That said, I've given up on cards in recent years. They get misplaced and disarranged in their box. They get taken out of the box and wander, sometimes jumping in the wastebasket when nobody's looking.

Next in usefulness is a loose-leaf book, although indexed address books often (a) have too little space for much information and (b) do not have enough section space in the ABC areas and too much in the XYZ area.

I do both journalism and press officer work and these days I have two books – one small format Filofax loose leaf book with an A-Z index which I carry wherever I go, and a larger loose leaf desk book of A4 lined paper into which I have inserted A-Z markers. In the Filofax are the names and numbers I consider most useful, and these are duplicated in the desk book which also has entries of lesser importance. I try to keep all my information up to date and I do not trust phone books – listings change, people go ex-directory, companies change names... all sent to try us!

It is also useful to have one prepared email address book section on your computer that will send releases to all your main users, thus avoiding typing out a whole list of recipients time after time. This should usually be reserved for 'one size fits all' occasions like an important appointment or resignation; elsewhere, as I have been at pains to point out, the value of 'tailoring' contributions to suit different publications or stations cannot be underestimated.

So much for the hardware...

Find the right man or woman for the job!

Said one editor I know, opening the post one day... 'Look, most of the lazy buggers haven't even taken the trouble to use my name.' All right, any journal carrying a section entitled 'Letters to the Editor' is likely to get letters addressed 'Dear Editor' or 'Dear Sir', or 'Dear Madam', but on reflection he has a point – media folk are people too, with names as well as positions. Much more to the point, if you find the person who is most likely to want to see your contribution, and thereafter communicate with them *using their name and position,* then you are on the way to building up a lasting rapport. Although a lot of what I am writing might sometimes seem like a rant about the things that piss off media people the most, this is far from the case. Trust me, people are grateful if you have done your homework, particularly in the area of names and positions.

How, though, do you find the right person? Simple. Ask. Phone up and ask who sorts out the editorial material. You might say, 'I have a press release – who should I send it to?' If the switchboard operator cannot help ask to speak to someone in the editorial department. Ask your target's name and position, and ask how to get in touch with them (extension number, plus all the other details listed below).

Entry details

Be extremely thorough. Note the proper address and postcode (some bloody-minded postmen have even been known to return letters not bearing a postcode), note the telephone number and extension, note mobile and after-hours numbers if appropriate, and note email addresses – on some busy papers everyone has their own dedicated email address.

If you like you can colour code everything, using coloured cards or highlighter pens to differentiate between, say, national and local newspapers. Though I've seen it done, I would say it's probably a step too far – after a bit you know your way around your own contacts book and the people and organisations dwelling therein like the back of your hand.

You will find it enormously helpful to double-list the target, say a newspaper, and the contact there who you deal with most often, and cross-refer the entries.

There are other things to find out on first contact and make notes about. What is the preferred method of sending contributions: by post or email? If the latter, what is the best software file format for sending written work? What is the file format for pictures, if you are sending any (or are likely to)? How much resolution is required (high quality is useful for magazine work, newspapers can often get away with fewer pixels but ridiculously small picture files are useless for reproduction in either). Would it be best to file words and pictures separately? Who deputises when your main contact is sick or on holiday?

Deadline details

Deadlines, the points beyond which nothing can be added, subtracted or altered in the publication or programme (short of recalling the publication or cancelling the broadcast time slot), are sacred cows throughout the media. If you deal with a limited number of targets you will in time learn their deadlines. The schedules are quite specific for the 'whole' production but newspaper editors often like material well ahead of deadline so that they can fill 'early' (inside) pages and leave the front and Page 3 (often referred to as the second news page, if not devoted to well developed young ladies) to last. Traditionally there also used to be a 'stop press' column for breaking news but this will rarely be your concern.

Broadcast editors also like to have much of their content completed ahead of the slot. Along with your contact details, jot down key deadlines for your targets but make a point of trying to supply your material early rather than up to the wire.

Define your own availability

Communication is a two-way trade. In all communications with your contact make it clear you are responsible for originating the material you are contributing and define your own availability should there be any queries or should the recipient want to seek further details – for instance, how they could contact the subject of a human interest story for some extra quotes, or perhaps to arrange a photograph. In making your first communication with your target you can ask them to put your details in their contact book.

In all of your written or emailed communications make sure you have your own contact details emblazoned loud and clear. If you are prepared to be available out of hours, or if you are often out and about and can only be reached on a mobile phone, give these details too.

But when you are off base or busy, beware answering snap inquiries that go further than your own remit to give out information on somebody else's behalf. If questions are asked that can only be answered by management, or by referral to files, say so – in a helpful way, of course: 'I'll make some inquiries. I (or someone) will get back to you on that...'

Add useful information as a footnote to your contribution

Media organisations often have a cuttings library to make it easy for reporting staff to dig out background to their stories. If you can save them time and effort by adding background material yourself they will be grateful. For example, the soap factory above always attaches to its press releases the helpful information that it is listed on the Stock Exchange, employs 170-plus staff drawn mainly from the Blighton area, and is located in the Fulton area of town where it operates from a former jam factory. It also notes the founder's name with a brief history of its growth. It states that a penny in the pound of all retail sales is donated to Third World aid, and explains that it sources all of its materials ethically and where possible from organic sources. Quite often these little points are picked up whenever stories sourced from a company press release are used in print or on the air.

As advised above, Press Officer Alison Key adds her own contact numbers here, together with an after-hours number (the Daily Westerner and many of the national newspapers interested in the rumoured takeover are put together by a shift working between 4pm and 1am).

Wisely, Alison has all this additional information, which she updates regularly if there are any changes, on a page stored in her computer: whenever she sends a press release she merely cuts and pastes the whole lot onto the end of her message before transmitting it.

Keeping in touch

Take every opportunity to talk to your contacts on a regular basis. Phone them from time to time. It is especially valuable to make a call shortly after sending out a press release, if only to make sure it has arrived safely in the correct recipient's hands. If it has, you can take the opportunity to ask if there are any initial queries. I advise that you don't also ask if your material is *going* to be used, or which edition it might appear in – it comes precious close to demanding attention in an area where others are best placed to judge the worth of the contribution.

Nobody, and I mean nobody, in the media world is ever able to give a cast-iron promise that any particular piece of material will be used.

Too many variables are in play when it comes to producing a

newspaper, a magazine or a programme. Console yourself with the thought that your contribution probably has as much chance as anything else of getting through – more of a chance, perhaps, after taking the advice in these pages. That said, there are plenty of press officers who say that persistent nagging pays off...

It certainly does often pay, however, to show an interest in your contact, providing they have the time to talk to you: how is the paper, magazine or radio station doing? Are there any major changes in policy, personnel? You can also thank them for their help in the past at this stage too, but try to avoid overt schmoozing.

As an 'after-care' measure all regular 'customers' deserve an annual Christmas card and if possible you should acquire a bunch of company cards for this very purpose. Even if they are ghastly pictures of the chairman's house with snow on the roof and his over-privileged kids making a snowman, it's the thought that counts! Needless to say perhaps, scribble your own thanks under the company message.

Seek feedback

It is perfectly in order to ask your contact for some feedback on your contributions, provided he or she is not busy. Avoid wasting time by trying to extract a long critique though, and go for simple questions: are my stories to long or too short? Is there enough information in them? Is there anything else you would like – more details, a picture perhaps? The crunch question of course would be whether or not your contribution is relevant to the publication or station concerned (or any use to it at all), but if you have done your research properly it should be and this is the one question you need not ask.

You can also call ahead of sending out a release to ask whether or not your recipients will be interested in its contents. Give some brief details of what it is about, and if you are including any exclusive information (details not being released to other likely recipients) make sure they know this, because it could swing the issue. Pre-checks like this can sometimes save you the bother of sending in a contribution or give you pointers about how your work can be adjusted to make it more acceptable. Such calls are also a good opportunity to check if you are running up against any deadlines.

It is generally *not* useful from your contact's point of view to ask why a contribution has *not* been used though it is tempting to seek this feedback and by and large it does no lasting harm. There are many circumstances that could bring this about – simple lack of space, for one. This frequently happens with small magazines and free newspapers where the advertising comes first and the editorial matter is a poor second cousin. Or (hard to believe I know) something more important might have cropped up – a major story demanding a splash on the front and six inside pages of background, perhaps. In the media world these circumstances are usually beyond an ordinary mortal's control. Things come up, situations change rapidly. If the station boss says he wants the whole of the news slot taken up with a scandal involving the local MP, everyone says 'Yessir!' and gets on with it. If this obliterates your carefully thought-out schedules and equally carefully crafted press handout, too bad – just lick your wounds and get on with the job. Especially don't berate anybody about it. Not even if it is a bitter blow to you. They won't thank you and it might have a negative effect on your future relationship.

Study your results

Elsewhere in this book I have noted that it is important to keep cuttings of your work, principally to show others that you are doing your job well (and perhaps to show to a prospective employer if you are changing jobs). However there is another good reason for keeping your work besides giving you a ready showcase: it gives you the opportunity to review the way in which it has been handled 'at the other end'. Here lie pointers to the preferences of the user – and valuable lessons in what you might contribute in the future. For example, if your work for one paper is regularly reduced to a couple of paragraphs, try sending them something in this form in future – pare it down to roughly the same format. Look out for style pointers too – more on this subject later in this book.

Look after your contacts, respect their professionalism, and the dividends for you will be greater.

After a time, it becomes perfectly clear what they want and what you should send them, and that makes all the difference between getting good coverage and blasting things off into the ether in the hope someone, somewhere, will respond.

Another 60 minutes and you'll be the greatest!

7

TELLING THE STORY

The maxim 'news is what people don't want you to know – all the rest is advertising' is a good one, if not strictly true. In fact you can put it on the same plane as 'never let the facts get in the way of a good story'. Both are funny, but both should not be deeply considered when contributing news material, and they shouldn't be taken as guidelines. Let others decide how close you *actually* come to advertising, and if any tinkering with the truth is going to be done, that's for others to carry out too – at least there's comfort in knowing and being able to prove that facts were facts when they left you, so far as it was possible to ascertain (it always pays to keep a hard copy, dated, of your work).

A much more valuable exercise comes with another maxim, 'study your market(s)'. Do. Make sure you regularly see copies of all the papers to which you contribute or to which you hope to contribute, and likewise watch or listen to relevant TV or radio programmes. And look (or listen) for the way contributors' work is treated.

If many one-paragraph 'in brief' columns are common, strive to send your lesser contributions in the same form; if longer, more interesting pieces are sometimes used, for example about executives taking new positions, seek to make your pieces 'fit' the same style and length.

First and foremost, though, make sure you have included all the relevant facts, all the points you want to get over. Often it helps to list these before you start to write a story.

The *minimum* length of a story is dictated by these facts. They are the skeleton, the bones, of what you write.

Let's start by looking at the things which get labelled as 'news' in an analytical fashion, later moving on to features. Somehow, your contributions have to fit one or the other of these categories unless they are simple diary items of a few bare words.

The category 'news' (which we have already decided is usually more properly called 'information') can be broken down into two further sections, 'hard news' and 'human interest'. This distinction does not matter too much for the moment as we first examine the construction of a story from its skeletal facts.

This is broadly the same ground that has to be covered by trainee journalists starting out their careers in journalism colleges or with a work placement and distance-learning package from a reputable trainer like the National Council for the Training of Journalists. The first thing the newcomer learns is that what looks like a fairly simple matter of telling a story is actually quite complex, mainly because of the underlying principles.

The first of these is that you are trying to attract and hold the attention of the reader or listener against the background of any number of alternative distractions that might at any moment make him put his paper down (perhaps never to pick it up again) or switch off his radio or television. This mythical reader is often given a name, 'The man on the Clapham omnibus', and you can just picture him on the top deck, being jostled by his neighbour who perhaps wants to chat, badgered for his fare money and perhaps catching the sight through the window of a mini-skirt out of the corner of his eye...

The headline in his paper is the first 'hook'. If it told the whole story the man on the Clapham omnibus would not bother to read on – yet that headline must intrigue, pull the eye, and give a hint of what is to come, be it a court report, a scandal, an accident, a disaster or whatever. But let's say it has done its job. Our bus passenger moves on to the introduction. This tightly written paragraph further involves him in the story telling the basic facts, usually explained to trainee journalists as answering a series of 'W' questions in a variety of orders: Who? What? Where? When? Of course, our reader also now wants to know 'Why?', and this is precisely the reason he is drawn into the rest of the story, which gives the background to the event or happening and any relevant comments from participants and onlookers. When facts, background and comment have run out, the story comes to a natural conclusion.

But in any newspaper there is an external factor at play too. The space available for editorial matter in any journal is finite (the action of providing news is often cynically referred to as 'filling the space between the adverts'), just as the time for a radio or TV news slot is finite. In constructing the story with the facts first, followed by the background and comment, the writer is also making it 'cuttable' from the bottom up – i.e. the lower material can be removed bit by bit, finally leaving only the facts if the story now needs to be moved to one side as a 'brief' to make room for a more important story. While this was particularly useful when newspapers were constructed from row after row of lead type, it is still helpful to retain this function of construction today. In the world of stories competing for newsworthiness on a page, every word has to justify its place.

The observant eye will also notice other design features in a printed paper which serve to make stories easy to read and assimilate. The width of the column is often quite narrow so that the reader does not have to move their head from one side to the other to scan lines. The introductory paragraph is in a larger type than the 'body' type which follows, accustoming the eye to the smaller print to follow. Not strictly relevant to writing press releases, I know, but nevertheless interesting.

To get back on track... however the format of the news story has evolved, it is here to stay – facts, followed by background, followed by comment (the last two not necessarily in that order). Now there are reporters (I can reveal after a lifetime in the trade) who cannot for the life of them write a story, particularly to this formula, but who nevertheless can dig out facts like a ferret searching for prey in a rabbit warren and also gather any amount of interesting quotes. Everything has to be rewritten for reporters like this – in that great play The Front Page, the newspaper has a 'rewrite man' (played by Jack Lemon in the film) who can turn bare facts to readable magic. In real life sub-editors fulfil this role. So, providing you get the facts down, your handout should be all right? Not necessarily. For a start, you are not as well known as the reporter who cannot write but is relied upon to deliver the facts, background and quotes in a jumble which can be sorted out by someone else. What you should strive for, therefore, is to put your contribution in the sort of shape expected of the main body of reporters – that standard story format of facts, background and comment.

This is actually the area where you might have the hardest battles with the organisation you represent, especially if your work is vetted by an official or, worse perhaps, by a committee. The official may have his own opinion of what is important (company bosses are often the hardest to convince that news of job cuts, for example, is more important than his views on the world accompanying the annual statement). If it's a committee, there may be many such opinions in play. There may be trouble ahead...

To start at the beginning, then, first muster your facts. Have the background to hand, and gather comments if warranted or necessary. Start to construct.

Headlines

It is not your job to create a newspaper style headline. It will without doubt be changed, replaced – your story's final position on the page will dictate the headline style and size and the strict number of letters each line must contain, give or take one or two. Filler items, you may notice, carry perhaps one line of 14pt in whatever font the newspaper fancies (to maintain the identity and overall look of the journal the choice of fonts used is usually very limited). Downpage items my warrant one or two lines of 24pt over two columns, more striking items 36pt across four or five columns, with types of 48pt and on up to 60pt or more reserved for the main 'lead' story on the page. Usually, especially in the 'red tops', the largest and slammiest types (sometimes called 'second coming' type) are reserved for the front page lead or 'splash'. All heading writers strive to include an active verb to imbue some liveliness and immediacy and catch the eye, including such famous examples as 'Nut screws washers and bolts' about a psychopathic rapist in a laundry and 'Eighth Army push bottles up Germans' about a famous battle engagement (Inadvertent, or were the sub-editors having a bit of fun? You decide!)

The press handout headline can be far less cleverly constructed but appeal should always be kept in mind because the recipient will undoubtedly be looking through a pile containing many other contributions. Consider the examples below about Blighton Soap introducing a new herbal line and perhaps taking on more staff to deal with this, starting with a simple 'label' heading:

New herbal product from Blighton Soap

and moving on to something more informative...

Blighton Soap expands production with herbal soap launch

and something much more 'newsy'...

Jobs hope in Blighton's magic soap

Now if you are an ordinary householder in the Blighton area, you probably buy your soap at Tesco, jumping at the four bars for the price of three offer. The first headline might be of passing interest, the second also, while the third might really be worthy of attention in a lot of households where youngsters and others are looking for jobs. It might also appeal to somebody with skin problems always on the lookout for a new miracle cure!

The local newspaper editors have to think much like the local population, put themselves in the place of their readers. Consequently while an editor's hand might hover over the first heading, the second one seems much more exciting – without it even having to be spelled out, any editor worth his or her salt will begin to ask if this scant information doesn't mean more local jobs. People like stories about employment chances and this will probably mean more newspaper sales. More sales means a higher circulation figure, and a higher circulation figure means you can charge more for advertising because you are reaching more people. That's the way it works.

The third heading is a clincher for our local editor, however. The facts are laid out for him, and he will have to act.

But beware: the same size definitely does not fit all. Certain homemaking magazines might be quite attracted by the first heading rather than the other two. To them, the prospect of more jobs in Blighton probably does not matter a jot, but lovely wholesome sweet-smelling Blighton Soap has much of a cachet in designer bathrooms. Readers will like to know about the new line. Also, Blighton Soap occasionally advertises with them – along with using the story the editor will probably tip off the advertising department to give the company's advertising agency a call.

Any takers for the middle headline? Of course ... what about trade papers dealing with household products, and even agricultural magazines serving the herb-growing areas with which Blighton Soap deals for its raw materials? Expansion in one field of industry often has a knock-on effect, likewise when factories close. Remember how many little companies making car seats, steering wheels and the like collapse when a car-maker goes under.

You see the shifts of emphasis? The wise press officer has a good think about headlines, and perhaps subtle shifts in contents for different recipients. However even if the rest of the handout might contain the same wording for every recipient, a few subtle changes to the way it is headed in each instance can alter its survival rate for the better.

Intros

Short for introduction – the first paragraph. Remember the Ws? Get the facts in – what is happening (or has happened) to whom (or what), and where and when did it all take place?

Try to make this as brief and snappy as possible:

> Blighton Soap founder and general manager Jill Stear announced today (Thursday April 9) that the leading UK soap firm is introducing an exciting new line of luxury herbal soap and hopes this will help it expand and employ more local people.

I must stress that there is absolutely nothing at all wrong with this introduction and any press officer could be proud of it. A curmudgeonly old sub-editor might well run his pencil thorough 'an exciting' and insert a simple 'a', because it remains to be seen how exciting the soap will be to its users, who after all are the real judges;

but hey, it's snappy enough as an intro and it contains all the basic facts.

A few more points, however, to bear in mind. First, is Blighton Soap a leading UK firm? Is the claim justified? If not, it will have to go at the editing stage. At least Blighton Soap hasn't gone the whole hog and pronounced itself to be 'Britain's leading soap manufacturer', in which case there could well be challenges from the likes of Lever, Boots or Cussons. In the past serious legal actions have arisen from such seemingly innocuous statements.

Second, some editors might query the necessity for Jill Stear to appear personally in the into. It could be made snappier without her.

Third, and a plus point this one, the press officer has seen fit to write the actual date of the announcement into the story. In this particular instance the date isn't critical; but there are occasions when it could be. If it's going in tomorrow's Advertiser it can be changed to 'yesterday', or in next week's Bugle to 'recently' rather than having to show that it is using last week's news (or perhaps it can be left out altogether by both papers, giving the impression that the announcement is contemporaneous). However if anyone has the need to refer back to the date of your original communication it can be pinpointed accurately:

> Since the company announced its new line on April 9...

And far more importantly, if you refer forward to any event, it's easy for people to work out this date in relation to the first one:

> Mrs Stear said the company would be starting job interviews at 9am on Monday morning.

The 'subbed' version of the intro could well now look like this (although I once again stress there is no reason to knock the original offering):

> As many as 50 more local jobs could be created after Blighton Soap announced a new luxury product.

followed by:

> Company bosses say job interviews could start as early as Monday...

But surely the first paragraph, the intro, has changed out of all recognition? Yes. But you must expect all intros to be changed rather than left in your wording. The Advertiser doesn't want to appear to be running exactly the same story with exactly the same wording as the Bugle, and vice versa. Intro tinkering, or 'putting a new nose' on a story is all part of the stock in trade of journalists.

Intros are usually between 16-30 words, rarely longer. In addition to being a quick second 'hook' when they appear in print, they are often in a larger type size than the rest of the story following, meaning there will be fewer words to each line. A wordy paragraph in large type makes many lines.

Further down the story, your writing can often survive more or less intact so long as it is not cut for pressure on space.

Faithfully reproduced quotes (see below) should never be tinkered with at all in story construction – beware of making people say or appear to say things they did not utter. It is in order, however, to 'jump' the uninteresting parts of a speech by omitting the words and inserting ellipses ...

> He said: "The new bicycle shed, referred to in paragraph 9 of the notes of the meeting of June 16 last, is nearing completion."

can become

> He said: "The new bicycle shed ... is nearing completion."

Actually, it is such a boring sentence you can take it out of quotes anyway:

> He said the new bicycle shed was nearing completion.

It's actually far better to give a paraphrase like this when you are unsure of the actual words spoken but can relay the gist of what was delivered. To repeat,

don't put words in people's mouths that didn't come out of them.

If you put quotation marks around anything, you are saying categorically that these were the exact words spoken.

(See also the notes on the placement of quotation marks a little further along in this chapter.)

The body

After delivering your facts you will have to flesh up the bones with more detail that you think will have interest for a reader (and we should always keep the reader, listener or watcher in mind)...

> Founder and current general manager Jill Stear said she was very excited about the herbal range which she expected to have wide appeal, particularly in today's health-conscious world.
>
> "Our herbalists have sourced many of the materials in locations like the Amazon and the Himalayas, where for centuries they have been used by native peoples for their skin care properties," she said.
>
> "We believe the market for this line is huge. It is definitely the biggest move we have introduced since the company was started.
>
> "Our premises in the former jam factory are now full to bursting and we may soon have to seek new premises. This new venture alone will hopefully mean at least 50 new jobs."
>
> The company's advertising agency is about to launch a major campaign on television and in the national press....

... and so on and so on for x-number of paragraphs (hopefully not too many more) to...

> ...Mrs Stear thanked loyal staff for helping the company grow to the extent that its future expansion was assured.
>
> "We have grown up with Blighton and Blighton people are the real heroes behind our success," she said.

You get the picture? Towards the end, the information is pretty slight and parochial. Nobody outside Blighton is going to be at all interested in this pat on the back for Blighton Soap's workforce, and although the Barton Evening News may run with these last snatches of information for its Blighton edition alone, other editions and the rest of the media will not give a hoot and the paragraphs will almost certainly be dropped.

With those final paragraphs our story about Blighton Soap's new line is probably as complete as it can be for the local press. Some other media outlets, while they might well cut out a fair bit of material, will not leave the story there. In the interest of making the story appear to be more 'their own' they may well seek extra quotes, usually via the press officer, enabling them to state:

> Mrs Stear told the Daily Westerner "this is the biggest advance in herbal soap for 20 years."

Financial papers and business sections might add information from the Stock Market:

> Blighton Soap's shares rose 10p on the news.

And home and beauty magazines (who might well have been sent samples of the new product along with the release) might also add a product review to their version of the report.

Just a few notes on the above before moving on.

Firstly, to her credit, our press officer has created something which cannot be ignored by a wide range of media outlets – it is a strongish news story, but subtly, it also presents a product to a big market, to potential sales. Free advertising? Without a doubt. More of this in a later chapter on tricks of the trade.

Secondly, she has stuck to clear, simple statements, avoiding management-speak like *'The Board of Blighton Soap is proud to announce...'*; or jargon, such as *'Ginkgo biloba extract is combined with podophyllum peltatum in a stereate base in a new soap product from Blighton Soap'*.

Quotes

The method of using double quotes around reported speech is fairly standard (but not universal) across the print media. After the phrase introducing the reported speech, a colon is usually employed (a comma will do but this is not so common), followed by the opening quotes. If the speaker is named after the quote, then the speech ends with a comma in front of the closing quote followed by the name. That comma can be replaced with a question mark in an interrogative quotation, or an exclamation mark if appropriate – again, in front of the closing inverted commas with the name following and a full stop.

Where quotes occur within quotes, it is common to employ single quotation marks to open and close the internal words or passage. Occasionally this makes things a little untidy towards the end of a paragraph but if you can't avoid it, don't. Consider the following example:

> "The biggest of the three men said: 'I'm going to bash you'," said Mrs Blair.

And where the reported speech spans more than one paragraph, it is common to place an opening quotation mark at the beginning of each paragraph but to omit a closing quotation mark at the end of the paragraph, until the end of the final quoted paragraph is reached (where the closing quotation mark is duly placed).

It is recommended this standard method is used in all handouts – see further notes on grammar later.

Although this is sometimes unavoidable in email transmissions,

try to avoid using generic quotation marks

...i.e. straight vertical quotation marks which are the same before and after quotations and take the place of 'proper' opening and closing quotation marks, with tails pointing up and forwards to open speech and down and backwards to close speech. Generics are very, very fiddly to replace, especially in a long piece. It seems even worse if generic quotes and proper ones are mixed as they sometimes are!

Applying the formula

So how does all this apply to organisations other than Blighton Soap? Let's take a look at a few, starting with our village W.I.

Here is a contribution Hilda Ronson has clattered out on her pre-computer sit-up-and-beg Olympus.

It went to Ambledown Parish News (via the vicar), Mrs Grogan who runs The Ambledowner which is slightly more racy than the Parish News, the Blighton Advertiser, the Blighton Packet, the Barton Evening News, the Daily Westerner, the Barton Today commercial radio station and the regional BBC radio and TV studios. Finding it increasingly difficult to source carbon paper locally, and to avoid typing the same material several times, Hilda uses the handy photocopier in the Post Office and Village Stores to duplicate her work.

```
Hilda Ronson, Dunroamin, Nettle Close, Ambledown BX7 7RA
Tel: Blighton 12345.

Ambledown W.I. March 7 2006

At the March meeting last night in Ambledown Village Hall
our speaker for the evening, Mr. Roger Jones, gave us a
very interesting and informative talk all about his
missionary work with the Amazon Indians and their marriage
ceremonies.
  He told us about his ten years in the Amazon backed up
with slides and afterwards he was thanked by our president
Mrs Marcia Briggs for a most interesting evening.
  Outgoing treasurer Elsie Tanner, who is retiring next
month, was thanked by Mrs Briggs and all general and
committee members for her five hardworking years of
service. She was presented with flowers and a tea cosy
knitted by Mrs Stewart.
  Mrs E. Harper, first, Mrs R. Jones, second, and Miss
Laura Ashley, third, won prizes for their flower arranging
judged by the vicar. The raffle was won by Mrs G. Peters
with number 279.
```

This was grand for the Parish News and the gossip sheet, which popped it into their pages without alteration. For a heading they used nothing more exciting than:

AMBLEDOWN W.I.

Once again, the Advertiser trimmed it to their 'W.I. roundup' formula of four rather tighter paragraphs, with a 'label' head:

Marriage in the jungle

AMBLEDOWN W.I. members learned all about the Amazon Indians and their marriage ceremonies at their March meeting.

> Roger Jones told of his ten years in the region. He was thanked by president Marcia Briggs for his slide show.
>
> Treasurer Elsie Tanner, who retires next month, was thanked for her five years of hard work in the post.
>
> Mrs E Harper, Mrs R Jones and Miss Laura Ashley won flower arrangement prizes. The raffle was won by Mrs G Peters.

Although she hasn't got this story reported elsewhere, Hilda is happy to have fulfilled her duty, as she sees it, of feeding her 'regulars' and getting some print space as a reward. Likewise her members and committee don't expect much else. They are glad of more cuttings for their notice board and archive.

However, Hilda might have had a bit of pre-publicity (the hall was only half full) if she had sent word, particularly to the local outlets, that Roger Jones was about to visit and talk about Amazon marriage ceremonies, and this would have been enhanced by any still pictures Mr Jones might have been able to supply showing him on location in Brazil interacting with indigenous people. People engaged in oddish activities and adventures in foreign parts are often worth writing about. It would be particularly appropriate if Mr Jones is a local man, living within the county or, better, in Barton, Blighton or even Ambledown itself. This would present an opportunity to invite the Blighton and Barton papers and perhaps even the Daily Westerner (and/or the broadcast media) to do a feature piece about Mr Jones and his travels, with a strong case for adding the footnote that his next engagement would be with Ambledown W.I. on such and such a date in March. Exploring the full possibilities of apparently ordinary proceedings are all part of the work – and the fun – of being a press officer.

Structure-wise, however, Hilda has hit the nail on the head – she has told everything in a straightforward fashion – earning two straight hits without alteration and a professionally 'subbed-down' piece, keeping her same order of contents, in a 'proper' newspaper. She has recognised the news value of her speaker above committee matters and the other details that crop up at every meeting (and the same person always seems to win that raffle!).

And what of the current news from Blighton Rangers?

We have already seen that Vicky Beckham (no relation!) has the regular duty of supplying 7-8 paragraphs (about 200 words) to the Blighton Advertiser and a little bit less – 150 words – to the Barton Evening News if the Rockets are playing a league game, which they are on this occasion with Hilltop United visiting from a small town at the other and of the county. In the true spirit of sportsmanship the Evening News has been rooting for Blighton Rangers for no other reason than that they are closer then Hilltop and a lot of Blighton supporters and townspeople in general have jobs in Barton.

Since she does not have a great deal of time on her hands Vicky first attends to her other duties of sending a scoreline to the broadcasters and the regional morning paper then sets about constructing her story for the Evening News. She aims to repeat this substantially for her Advertiser report but commendably hopes she can 'tweak' it a bit beforehand so that both reports are not exactly the same. She writes to the Advertiser ordered length because she knows the Evening News can cut it back to suit their purposes.

Both papers incidentally pay her 'lineage' for her contributions: around 6p a published line of text, which can add up to a bit of pocket money in the season. She drew this fact to the attention of club officials and asked if it should be given to club funds but the manager said he was happy for her to keep the small 'perk'. Such benefits rarely come a press officer's way!

The game is not a good one for Blighton – in fact the home team goes down 2-5 and to make matters worse their top striker is badly hurt. They didn't even score in the penalty shot that arose from this incident!

Vicky heads her piece:

Rangers go down 1-5 in league clash

and her report follows:

> Blighton Rangers lost by five goals to one in the league match quarter final replay against Hilltop United at the Barton Road ground last night

(Thursday March 22) in a match which always seemed to go Hilltop's way.

Playing uphill at the start and against an increasing wind, Blighton nevertheless scored the first goal – a blistering shot from 25 yards by David Edwards – and fans revived the hope that they could take this vital quarter final game.

It was not to be, however – first Hilltop's Richard Grant and then Wayne Griggs were able to run virtually unchallenged to within striking distance and both shots beat keeper Colin Jones.

Starting the second half 2-1 down was bad enough but within two minutes Edwards was flat on the ground nursing his ankle after a collision in the Hilltop penalty box. The Rockets were awarded a penalty for this but Mike Ellison's shot went wide.

Hilltop were soon on the attack again and despite gaining the wind advantage a dispirited Blighton side let them through for three more successful goal attempts. It did not help to hear that Edwards, who was stretchered off, would not play again for the rest of the season.

"Losing our chance of winning the league in this vital game was bad enough but without Edwards we will really begin to slip in the table,'"said coach Tim Walsh.

"It is back to the drawing board for us. Our only hope now is to train hard through the summer, get everyone fit and make a better fist of it next season."

That's about 260 words, and off it goes ... Vicky hasn't any more time to meet the inside sports page deadline for tomorrow's early edition, so can't fiddle about chopping words. It's a thoroughgoing report and she's quite proud of it.

Next morning she finds in the News, under a head:

Edwards hurt as Rockets hopes fizzle

Coach Tim Walsh conceded Blighton had lost all hope of league glory as they crashed 1-5 to Hilltop in a quarter final replay that saw striker David Edwards badly hurt.

"Losing our chance in this vital game was bad enough but without Edwards we will really begin to slip,' he said. 'It is back to the drawing board."

Playing uphill against wind, Blighton scored the first goal – a blistering shot from 25 yards by Edwards.

However Hilltop's Richard Grant and Wayne Griggs were then able to run in unchallenged to beat keeper Colin Jones twice.

Two minutes into the second half Edwards was floored. The

> Rockets were awarded a penalty but Mike Ellison's shot missed the target.
>
> Hilltop went on the attack again and dispirited Blighton let them through for three more goals. It did not help to hear that Edwards was out for the rest of the season.

Now here's an example of a sub-editor working for his keep and not only trimming something to the required length but also retaining its essence.

He has also managed to swizzle the story round to somehow give it more immediacy than the 'real time' blow-by-blow account submitted by Vicky. And yes, in this instance the quotes have been moved nearer the top of the story *for that very purpose*. The analysis of the game, if you like, has taken over from the event itself.

As for Vicky – well, she's certainly not dismayed her story has been changed around a bit. She's quite used to this. Besides, she can now submit her original piece to the Advertiser with a clear conscience and without any further work!

She has also learned to look for other 'saleable' points in match stories. Edwards' injury is worth a paragraph in the Daily Westerner and she has tipped off the broadcasters who mention it in their sports roundups together with Vicky's results. One of the nationals that also occasionally takes material from her will run a paragraph. She is thinking of contacting a soccer magazine later in the year to ask if they want a piece about David Edwards' recuperation and future playing prospects – if this is used, she will be paid more than a bit of lineage.

Three stories, many outcomes

There you are then, three approaches where the story construction process has more or less worked, though not always in a predictable way. Is it worth making the effort? Don't answer until you have seen how badly thought-out and poorly constructed handouts fare in the following chapter, 'How *Not* to Do It'.

8

HOW *NOT* TO DO IT

Underkill

Blighton Town Council has always had to go for the cheapest possible approach to practically everything, and this includes putting out information about its activities. When it comes to spending which translates directly into council tax charges, district and county councillors who make sure such decisions are invisible. Not so town councillors who walk Blighton's streets, go to the pubs, go to church there – the fear of the lynch mob must always be upon them.

The Town Clerk interprets 'media relations' as sending out the minutes, decisions and reports of various committees, and that is about it. He is authorised to buy advertising space for statutory notices on which there is a legal requirement to publish the information they contain. Without a town crier and a news-sheet of its own, the clerk places advertisements in the Advertiser, which he sees as a 'bona fide' newspaper as against the 'free' Bugle. From time to time the free's advertising reps ring up and point out that their paper is seen by more people for less cost but he remains inflexible on this point. It is the way the council has always done things.

He assumes that the minutes are doing their job because minuted notes about such things as switching on the town's Christmas lights do often lead to stories appearing in one local paper or another. Recently, too, there was a report and picture featuring the retirement of the long-serving council-employed gardener who looks after the town park and boating lake. His imminent departure and a farewell party for well-wishers and colleagues had been similarly noted in minutes.

Little did he know that in the case of the Christmas lights the town's zealous Chamber of Trade had urged the press to attend the occasion, while the retirement of the municipal gardener had been flagged up for the media by some of the man's pals. The publicity had little if anything to do with Town Council minutes. Bland and sketchy, like a black hole little light ever escapes from this source.

On the one occasion the Clerk had chosen to be proactive, the results had not been at all encouraging. The following was sent out with the usual round-robin batch of minutes.

> *The press is invited to send representatives to a function in which the Mayor, Colin Hanbury, will open a new youth facility at the lake end of the recreation ground. Details or request from the Town Clerk.*

That's a press handout?

Unhappily, the town youth club and the enthusiastic youngsters who had brought about the construction of this very welcome facility had been given an assurance by the town council (which contributed £100 to the Lottery-supported venture) that the Town Clerk would arrange the publicity.

The result, predictably, was a rather embarrassed little gathering involving the civic bods on one side, youth representatives on the other, a couple of parents and absolutely no media representatives. The sin of omitting that the 'facility' involved skates was the worst part of the clerk's 'publicity' strategy. That one word alone might have alerted journalists to something with pictorial possibilities. Also, since the town youth are always complaining that there is little for them to do except mooch about and annoy people, it would have rung a few bells as to the possibility of a positive story to redress a sea of negative ones. As it was, who the devil could ascertain what was going on? Certainly there is too little information for a news editor to commit a reporter or a photographer to the event. Worse, a scant two sentences were easily overlooked.

A photograph taken by one of the parents who had brought a digital camera along to the occasion did appear a week later in the

Bugle, but quite a good opportunity to trumpet what the town was doing for its youth had by then been lost.

Buried news

By contrast there is real news in the following offering from Barton gas and Electricity. The trouble is, it is buried well down in the communication which has gone out as a 'round robin' to everybody, local and national alike, as is Tony Williams's habit. It has gone through a few drafts, having been well picked over by the board before being approved for release. Tony doesn't question any of the changes he has had to make. His is not to reason why. That way, everyone is pleased except the people outside the firm – his recipients. Also if there are any comebacks he's not the one to blame!

Lower dividend for BGE shareholders

The Barton Gas and Electricity Board has announced a slight fall in shareholder dividends for the half-year ending September 31 following a 1.5 per cent fall in gross profits compared with the same period last year.

The profit shortfall, attributed to customers being more conscious of energy-saving in the current uncertain state of the national economy, as well as steeply rising natural gas prices, was partially offset by the early onset of autumn cold weather which saw surges in demand on the coldest nights.

Chief Executive Sir Paul Beard said he wanted to assure shareholders that the company was doing everything it could to maintain operating profits while cutting down production costs.

"Compared with other utility companies in this field Barton Gas and Electricity is a strong performer, particularly in sales of natural gas, where we have negotiated a long-term deal for stable prices with Siberian company Biggasco," Sir Keith reported to the Board.

"As a result of market pressures there will be a short term cut in our interim dividend paid this half year, but future growth looks assured and I have every confidence in our prospects for the next half-year."

The Chief Executive said he would like to assure business and domestic customers that the company was doing everything it could to keep its prices competitive in an extremely volatile market.

In other points the board heard that regrettably some of the rising costs would have to be passed on to most consumers. However substantial savings were being made in salaries with a considerable reduction in head office staff.

The board approved a 15 per cent half-year bonus for Sir Keith and fellow executives.

Now while share and stock exchange news is certainly important to the people who own shares, BGE has many more local employees than there are local shareholders, and it also has thousands of consumer customers across the nation – since deregulation, companies like this have outgrown a purely 'local' role.

Remember the maxim that everyone mentioned in a report is a potential reader/listener/viewer? In the middle of Tony Williams' release is a good story for the financial pages in the tie-up with the Russian supplier, while at the bottom of the release three quite juicy facts have been 'buried'. One is the fairly obvious point that BGE's prices are about to rise, and the other is that there are clearly a lot of job cuts in the pipeline.

And last but not least, why are all the execs getting a good pay rise while everybody else appears to be suffering? (Cue for violins, 'It's the rich wot gets the pleasure.')

OK, you can argue that despite putting things upside down (a matter largely out of his control, though he has learned by now to 'read' the way the board likes things to be presented), Tony (or the board) has actually got across everything people need to know.

Remember 'news is what people don't want you to know'? Here it's spelled out (and see the chapter later on about bad news days).

Like it or not, these points will catch somebody's eye and spark further enquiries. Better by far to state them up front, even if in Tony's case this means confronting his board with some uncomfortable facts, principal of which is that the truth will out.

In efforts to minimise the bad news by giving it a scant mention the board may well be doing themselves one (or three) in the eye. What if there are mitigating circumstances, for instance, for all these apparent injustices? Job cuts, for example, can be carried out quite bloodlessly by waiting for people to quit the firm or retire (the term often used is 'natural wastage'). The price rises hinted at may be well below the rises being considered by other players in the field. Sir Keith might have steered millions of pounds worth of new business the company's way, or he might have taken over the tasks of several people who left the firm.

I'm not saying that every cloud like the ones mentioned has a silver lining, but there are often stories behind stories that deserve to come out. Why not get them into the open at once? That way things are done and dusted quickly, while evasions on the other hand tend to hang about and the media has its suspicions aroused and starts to make its own investigations.

One of Tony's less serious faults is that he avoids putting out human interest stories about company employees and special events that can give firms a cosier image to their customers and the public at large, such as: a company Easter Bonnet day, where everyone paid to wear silly clothes, that raised £250 for the local hospice; a Christmas party collection that raised cash to keep the local air ambulance flying; an employee who has raised 50 foster children; the service engineer who rushed a pregnant customer to hospital in the nick of time to give birth, and so on and so on.

Although he has a full time job Tony isn't required to do any more than he does. Actually he's looking forward to retirement. With his replacement, the company could well get a better deal.

Overkill

Blighton Folk Museum and Gallery's owners undertake all their own publicity work.

Remember, despite its title this is a largely commercial concern. As mentioned in a previous chapter, they have learned not to expect to see all the details they send out in their handouts faithfully reproduced: although they submit details of opening times, ticket prices and concessions, these are often disappointingly replaced in the media with wording like '*full details from the museum*'. From a newspaper's point of view, giving such details is free advertising, and this is particularly true of the 'free' paper that relies entirely on advertising revenue. Also, if a paper includes such details for one firm it has an apparent duty to provide the same service for everyone. The museum owners keep up their pressure by giving every possible detail, in spite of knowing this is 'overkill' and the best way to make the most of publicity is to run a detailed advert in the same edition to bolster the scant materiel that makes its way into the news pages. They also call their press contacts often to try to get a vow that some pre-event material is used, but no newspaper will promise to run *any* contributed material whatsoever (in case something more newsworthy comes along to take its place), let alone run it beside an advertisement. However, this is frequently another plea the Museum folk make, unaware that they are asking for more advertising space at absolutely no cost. Who can do that? Nobody in their right mind.

A study of what is and what is not acceptable in terms of detail would save them a bit of work. So would seeking some head-to-head feedback from their media contacts. But as enterprising people they keep trying it their own way. Someday, somehow, something will surely get through!

A compromise the museum has reached of late is to run a 'free tickets' campaign in association with the free newspaper, an arrangement which suits both parties (see the later chapter covering this subject).

Meddlers! Beware!

Whatever organisation you work for, within it there is usually someone who does not approve of the way you do things and perhaps has the idea that they could do better themselves. These people often feel what you are doing is a piece of cake, money for old rope. Beware – ten to one they want your job!

The example of Tony Williams' 'handouts by committee' is an outstanding example of the folly of letting others direct what you know to be the best way of handling a story. This is a sense that grows with experience. By all means take advice and listen to what everyone has to say, particularly those superior to you. Be prepared to argue your reasons for presenting things in your own way and in the final analysis use your own judgement. The longer you are in the job, the more clout you will find you have!

One senior writer I know is a dab hand at producing advertising features – an area where the advertiser does indeed have a say over what goes into the 'copy' since they are paying for the space it occupies. His modus operandi (an approach shared by most people who do similar work) was to jot down the facts then weave them into a positive piece of work that would get the advertiser's customers practically battering down the door to buy their goods or services. One day it was clear he was becoming exceedingly irritated with a butcher who was demanding to see every draft of the feature after making change upon change. 'Look,' said the elderly journalist finally running out of patience. 'I don't tell you what to put in your xxxxing sausages so you needn't try to tell me how to write my feature!'

While it is not a good idea to ruffle feathers quite this thoroughly, it is not a bad policy to make clear exactly where you stand!

9

PRESENTATION

Dreadful or helpful?

The subject of presentation is important. It's how you make your first and often vital impression on your target, usually someone in the role of news editor, copy-taster or sub-editor.

Apart from the cosmetic aspect of a good-looking job you will also earn brownie points by making your contribution as easy as possible for the recipient to understand, treat and use.

Does this mean that giving your news release a big slammy headline and throwing at it the full capability of your font applications, perhaps even liberally dotting the work with Clipart thingumajigs and smiling animated homolocons? Far from it.

In one of my freelance news editing jobs I have to groan whenever I sight work from several contributors, but one in particular stands out above the rest. Unfortunately the material he sends out about the preparations, running and aftermath of a large public music festival is unavoidably useful.

Not only does Mr X employ all the devices mentioned above in his email transmissions, but he also takes full advantage of everything else his computer has to offer: coloured type, the ability to emphasise words by making them bold, italic or underscored, and as a final blow he often delivers some of the words entirely in capital letters whether or not they are worth highlighting at all. He has even been known to go one step further and alter the between-line and paragraph spacing, and of course he invariably uses 'generic' apostrophes or quote marks rather than 'proper' ones that embrace the start of a word or passage with forward pointing tails and finish with backward pointing ones.

I can only be thankful that I have to deal with his work on a computer because hard copy like this would of course need retyping in plain type before it could be marked up to go to the printer.

I can change some of these emailed sins more easily than others simply by highlighting the whole job and changing it to the typeface (font) and type size I want, at the same time removing the spurious emphasis gizmos. Then I can do a 'find and change' on the punctuation and I can get the right spacing with a couple of hits, but there is nothing at all I can do with the unnecessary words in caps except retype each and every one.

As a result, I am sure you can see, I hate a job from Mr X (nice fella, don't get me wrong, but he can never see any reason in my complaints and he might be the first person to get a free copy of this book from me). Knocking an ordinary unfussy news release into shape might have taken a couple of minutes, but his often takes several minutes. Tedious when you have a lot of material to shift for an edition. And so unnecessary when you also know that Mr X's actual words, style and grammar – without the additional nonsense – are perfectly usable when given just a few tweaks. They could almost go straight into print.

There are separate requirements for hard (typed) and email copy, though we can start with some generalisations.

For all copy

By all means get the company heading on the work – in emails or with a pen that can be erased at a stroke – but take it from me, if you don't want the image of a man or woman close to a coronary attack haunting your dreams of a night, keep it simple. This applies to hard copy as much as it does to an electronic transmission.

A recognisable font (Times, Helvetica, or even Courier to mimic key-thumped typescript) and a size of around 12 point is ideal. Smaller is a chore to read, but you can go marginally larger, say 14 point, before you start shortening the number of words in each line to a ridiculous degree – that makes the story cover much more space and begins to nark the recipient.

Make sure you have given contact details for yourself or someone else who can take queries. Anonymous copy will never be used by anyone. An out of office hours number or a mobile number is also useful – especially for papers that are 'put to bed' in the small hours of the morning. Chances are you won't be woken from your slumbers to explain something in your copy but it has happened. What you have contributed is first and foremost your responsibility.

Presenting hard copy

Newsrooms do not have the volume of hard copy – the term for typed material sent by post or fax – that they used to, though it is still a considerable quantity. But the rise and rise of email communications to the media was inevitable once the technology 'escaped' into the wider world from the situation in which it was used mainly by scientists and academics to communicate at distance. Once it was seen that 'copy' could be stripped from emails by cut and paste and attached documents and digital pictures could be dragged onto anybody's desktop, there was no limit to the delight this gave to newsrooms. More about this below. Still, though, the typed release is very much a part of news-gathering and it helps the contributor, you the press officer, to know how typed copy ends up in print so that you can see how the actual layout of your typed page makes it much more acceptable to a reader and end-user.

Hard copy contributions inevitably have to be retyped at some point in the publishing process. They are either 'keyboarded' into an electronic publishing system by a typist from where they can have further treatment by an editor, or they are 'marked up' for a printer or rewritten by a journalist or sub-editor who picks out the gist of the communication.

Computer terminals might have taken the place of clattering typewriters and the smell of molten lead and printing ink might no longer pervade newsrooms (few journals of any kind can afford to have their own presses on the premises these days), yet newsgathering remains an exciting operation. Everything is still geared to getting words into print (or on the air), often against the clock. That keeps the people involved living on their wits. Usually they will have staff reporters and feature writers as well as relying on contributed material. All of this now has to be edited so that it hits the reader (or listener) in a digestible and hopefully attractive form. That usually means the next stage in the process is editing, and the people who do this are called 'sub-editors' to make sure they are not confused with the figurehead editor – the head honcho (though there are still working editors who get their hands dirty).

Sub-editing (or 'subbing') is highly skilled work. Firstly, the 'sub' must make your words fit into the allocated space on a page design created by a layout sub or perhaps a chief sub editor. Often this means it has to be cut to a predetermined number of words; reducing the type size is not an option because this would make a page messy or confusing. Further, the story must be grammatical and it must, in the case of print at least, fit the 'style' of the journal. I have written more about style later but just to illustrate the concept, it is possible to write percentages as, say, 2 per cent, 2 percent or even 2%, and there needs to be a house rule so that stories side by side do not have different words or symbols. Does that really matter? Probably not in many instances but it can give rise to confusion, with the reader wondering if '%' means something different to 'percent' or 'per cent'. You are in more trouble with a policeman (not really I hope!) who can be represented by 'Pc' with a small 'c', 'PC' or P.C.' (also confusable with personal computers and parish councils) or even 'constable', 'con' or 'const'. This does *not* matter to the contributor over much, of course, but do be on the alert for inconsistencies in your own writing if you want to be taken as a professional. You do, don't you? If you have one journal to which you regularly contribute, it helps to get to know their house style – you might even ask if they have a style guide (sometimes called 'The Style Book') that they can send you or email to you. Some papers adopt style books published by organisations involved in journalism training or those used by prominent papers – the style books of The Times and The Economist are famous examples and you can if you wish download gems like the 1928 'Style-book of the Manchester Guardian' in pdf format via the link www.guardian.co.uk/styleguide/0,,184913,00.html.

A trawl of websites can turn up many more examples.

More on this subject later. To return to 'subbing', hard copy is sometimes 'marked up' in pen or pencil for a printer or compositor (a rare breed in this electronic world) with corrections and alterations clearly marked, the 'body' type font and size required, the heading likewise with its type size and font detailed, notes on any picture which accompanies the story plus a caption, and a 'catchline' on each paper sheet which enables body, heading, picture and caption, often created on different machines, to be 'married' or collated before it goes into the page. Obviously with the advent of Desktop Publishing (DTP) all the stages above can be dealt with on-screen, and often one person alone (depending on the size of the publication) can adequately perform all the functions.

When you are sending hard copy ensure it is double spaced for ease of reading and to leave room for any alteration marks. Likewise leave good wide margins each side and top and bottom for the same reasons.

With hard copy, it is perfectly acceptable to put your own heading on the work so long as you do not imagine this will survive the publishing process intact – the sub-editor will undoubtedly be given a heading style and size, say for example two lines of 24pt Tempo Bold across two columns, which will have an inflexible number of letters or characters for expressing the gist of the story.

Like everything else in this creative process, headline writing is an art that need not concern the contributor too much. Imagine, though, a newspaper in which the headlines told you so much about the stories that you did not need to read the text, or contrary to this, one whose headlines were so dull you cannot see any point in reading the story at all. The headliner's job is to excite interest with a hint of what is to follow.

If you are adding a picture (see the chapter on pictures) you will need a caption explaining what is going on and who is involved. Try to name everyone in the picture and double check their names – giving 'Davis' instead of 'Davies', 'Dennis' instead of 'Denis' or 'Rachel' instead of 'Rachael' may not seem to be much of a sin to you, but try to remember how annoyed you get when someone spells your name wrong, especially in something so public as the pages of a newspaper or magazine. The journal will be expecting you to give them the right names and may not have the time to check for themselves. And newspapers love names. The chances are that anyone with their name (particularly with a picture, and whether for a good reason or infamy) in the paper will go out and buy at least one copy, maybe more. So, perhaps, will their mum, gran, husband or wife and so on and so on. That means sales, and sales are the key to two revenue streams, from advertising and cover price. Your checklist, then for sending *hard* copy:

- Use a clear, unfussy typeface the equivalent in size and clarity of a standard typewriter (traditionally Courier, but Times and Helvetica are equally acceptable)
- Double space the main text
- Make sure copy is dated; include your own contact details.

Presenting electronic copy

Whether by email, CD ROM or (becoming rare) floppy disc, the press officer or contributor should use recognisable popular word processing software that can easily be translated by either Apple Mac or PC/Windows-using recipients. To date most of the print media have chosen Mac platforms with Quark Express as the DTP programme of choice; however, these companies are well aware that PCs and Word for Windows are more popular in the wider world and all have arranged compatibility between the two systems.

Emails can be sent either as a simple 'body' email or an attachment provided they are in a simple and openable form. Usually Word files are openable on Mac and Microsoft platforms, and Apple files are also openable in Windows or text file applications.

Avoid PDFs entirely

for press and PR work unless they simply provide additional information or a bit of background; while they may be openable and completely readable what matters is the ability to 'strip' them of usable pieces of type. Without specialised software which is by no means in universal use, it is impossible to 'get into' PDFs. Any info gleaned from them has to be retyped from the screen – extra time-consuming work as well as an area for making copying mistakes.

Avoid also sending files using specialised software

such as Microsoft Publisher (.pub files) or other Microsoft applications which are not in general use, however handy you find them for your own work.

Do heed the note above about keeping to a simple font such as Helvetica or Times, with a decent readable size (12pt, 14pt), in black and without highlights, heavy caps, colours or underscores for extra emphasis. You are sending them to experts who know the weight of words.

Likewise avoid tinkering with the between-line spacing and the before and after paragraph spacing.

Keep text and picture files separate. While it is possible to embed pictures with text in some computer programmes it makes extra work for the recipient to separate them and separate them they must: there is probably not one picture in any paper which has not been Photoshopped to adjust tone, colour and contrast to make it suitable for printing. Thus let your jpg or tif files accompany your words as attachments and, as with the text, avoid any obscure forms of picture file to make life easy at the receiving end. If you are sending a lot of picture files chop them up into batches of twos or at the most threes to send. This avoids them bouncing back if too much data is heading into the recipient's computer, as well as avoiding lengthy download times.

If you have Photoshop or its equivalent yourself it is best to avoid tinkering with images before you send them off to the media – apart from often making the files much bigger by adding more bytes of information, altering images that are going to be published can be dangerous. More about this later in the chapter on pictures.

A checklist for electronic copy, then:

- clear large font (12pt Helvetica or Times)
- no need to double space
- send as in-line text or Word attachment
- avoid obscure word processing files and PDFs
- keep pictures and text separate
- make sure your copy or the event referred to is dated
- add contact details – phone numbers as well as email addresses.

10

DO IT WITH STYLE

Releasing surplus apostrophes at the end of the day

Style, fairness and grammar

Not another English lesson, I can hear you say! Well, OK – but perhaps you can look at it not as a refresher on all that tedious stuff you put behind you when you left school, but an opportunity to look with fresh eyes into a world where use of language is very much the currency of day-to-day life and where everything is geared to giving the reader, listener or viewer an immediate and easy-to-understand picture of the world around them.

The world of news presentation is a place where the simple clear sentence and unambiguous statement hold sway over lengthy discourses and explanations; where every word has to justify its being allowed to take up space, be that in print or in airtime.

Unless we are talking about weighty articles by experts in the heavier broadsheets, short sentences are the clearest and quickest way to convey information. Sentences with lots of qualifying clauses on the other hand bog the reader down, and can make them lose the thread before they are halfway through – especially if there are other distractions. Remember the man on the Clapham omnibus?

Likewise sentence inversions and unnecessary convolutions interrupt a straightforward read. Not for nothing do newspaper offices keep a 'black book' of cuttings showing, among other things, ambiguous headlines that have crept into print unnoticed. With them are other little bits of nonsense: an 'intro of the week' competition, for the story introduction most likely to confuse or bore a reader, likewise a 'longest sentence of the week' section.

The serious side of all this is to identify bad practice, and keep everyone on the alert.

One of the most common sins is killing reader interest with a dull piece of writing.

Compare for example:

> It started off as an ordinary rainy Monday in Chipping Sodbury High Street this morning with townsfolk going about their usual business... the smell of bread wafted from the bakery, people called by at the newsagents for their daily paper...

with:

> A violent explosion rocked Chipping Sodbury High Street this morning and left a scene of devastation in the rain.

...which facts the writer was going to get around to two or three paragraphs down the story!

That first approach might be all right for a fairy tale. In the real world of journalism the motto is 'tell it like it is', and that means getting straight to the facts and not fannying around.

Lessons here for the Press Officer? Of course. The first one is to keep the writing as tight as possible and be ruthless about omitting extraneous facts whatever the temptation to embellish a tale.

First, though, let us to return to a subject touched upon earlier, that of 'style'.

Putting on the style

'Style' in a newspaper sense does not mean 'airs and graces' as it might in the outside world, but rather 'the way we do things here'.

Style points can be as various as the way a police constable is abbreviated (PC, P-C, Pc, Con, Const to name but a few) to whether the heir to the throne is called Prince Charles, the Prince of Wales or the Duke of Cornwall... or anything else.

One of the main reasons for this is to maintain consistency throughout the publication, and not have stories side by side (in an extreme case) that have different versions leading to confusion for the reader – e.g., is that PC the same thing as the Pc next door, or are we looking at different ranks (assuming the context makes it clear both are policemen, and one is not a Parish Council or a Personal Computer)? A worse scenario is having alternatives of abbreviations like this in the same story. Whenever a journalist joins a new publication they are schooled in its style requirements. Usually they are given a copy of the 'style book' to study and keep by them. As well as abbreviations spelling points are covered, for example when to use '-ise' as opposed to '-ize' endings when creating verbs from words like 'random', or whether to stick with one version or the other entirely. Once you start looking you can find many spelling dilemmas or quandaries – for example whether to write 'medieval' or 'mediaeval', and so on and so on.

Now on the face of it, it doesn't matter a hoot to a contributor how variable terms, spellings and abbreviations are used, because surely the recipient can change the contributed copy to suite their particular taste? Quite so.

However, remember you are trying to be helpful. The helpful contributor's helpful copy earns points, and points mean prizes in the form of getting copy into print or on the air. And while you may not be able to tailor your copy to the style points of each individual recipient, you can make sure that it is consistent in your own stories. That makes it easy to identify and change if necessary to the recipient's own style, and if this is in electronic form it is a simple find-and-replace operation that can zap every occurrence in the transmission in one operation.

Of course if you have a recipient who takes a large amount of your work you might take the trouble to learn their style in preference to the style points of lesser recipients: a request to the news editor will often get you a copy of their particular style book in print or electronic form (a web search will give you several style book sources for a variety of leading publications).

Style matters less with writing for radio and TV but all the same it has to metamorphose into speech via a written form, and it's here where consistency matters the most.

Let's pass on to some other areas where writing press releases is a different task from other types of creative writing. Some are to do with balance and fairness towards the subjects, i.e. the people being written about, which might not concern the press officer overly, but are nevertheless well worth learning about. Others are to do with constructing words in an easily digestible form, moving on from the points in the last chapter about keeping things simple.

Balance and fair reporting

Much justified criticism on the grounds of harming inter-race relations has come the way of journalism in recent years. For instance, the mention in a story of a person's skin colour or racial origins, if it has no bearing on the narrative, cannot be justified under any terms. Nor is there any place for recording real social disadvantages such as a nasty case of acne if there is no apparent reason for doing so. Descriptions like 'tall' or 'pretty' are less socially sensitive but again inclusion is questionable when you consider their opposites (which you certainly would not use), unless there is clearly a case for their use, as in '*luckily Mr Jones was tall enough to lift the kitten down from the branch*'.

Generally best avoided then, likewise 'fat' even if circumscribed as 'overweight', and 'thin' or 'underweight' or even 'anorexic'.

Trainee journalists are usually advised to apply one final criterion to any story that is critical of any individual or group, and this is the question they are told to ask regardless of whether or not everything in the story is true and completely accurate:

Is it fair?

Asking this question could, for example, stop a reporter mentioning a relatively minor misdemeanour such as parking on a double yellow and destroying somebody's life by earning them the sack from their job as a chauffeur. The driver ought to have had better sense but who has really been harmed by his transgression?

Balance is another consideration when writing a story. Every story has two sides, and it is the media's duty to give both sides. There are circumstances where this can be initially unavoidable, for example a story criticising the local health authority where it has been impossible to get a quote (which may or may not rebuff the criticisms) from the manager before an edition deadline. However every step should be taken to make sure the manager's views are known in a subsequent (follow-up) report.

The bones of the story below which I first used when writing the NCTJ's *Guidelines for Correspondents* illustrate what the balance thing is all about.

> Gary Swinger, a trapeze artiste, has enjoyed top billing in circuses all around the world, yet an approach to the manager of the leisure centre in his home town to use the magnificent new facilities for workouts is turned down.
>
> Swinger takes his gripe to the press – there are many other people using the facilities, he says, so why should he be discriminated against?
>
> He goes even further and says that apart from being small-minded the manager is turning his back on a wonderful opportunity to do some good for the youth of the town. If he, Swinger, could use the facilities for regular practice, he would be prepared to give training and advice to youngsters wishing to learn his skills. He adds many towns throughout the world have been happy to give him the use of their recreation halls – for which he pays good money – without a quibble.
>
> Now a reporter who prepares a report on these facts alone has a one-sided story. What does the manager say in answer to Swinger's attack? Without his thoughts on the subject there is no fairness, no balance. It does indeed look as if he is small-minded, maybe even irrationally mean.
>
> As it happens in this case the manager's comments are sought. He says he is very sorry to disappoint Swinger. He sympathises with his position but in any matters that might put undue stress on the hall structure – and this appears to be one of them – he first has to seek

permission of the town council to have the matter referred to the architects. In fact he has put this in train. Once everything is inspected and approved he would be overjoyed to welcome Swinger.

This time the story *is* balanced, and complete – and nothing has been taken away from it by obtaining the other point of view (but fearing this will be the case often stops many reporters from taking their enquiries too far). Swinger has had his grouse and the grouse has been countered, it makes a nice little story and everyone is happy.

Had the manager instead told the reporter he had no comment whatsoever to make on the situation, this fact too could have been recorded in the story to 'balance' it – 'no comment' in fact being a very strong comment in its own right. Obviously in that event the manager comes over as a Jobsworth, even a latter-day dictator placing himself above talking to the press. The reader can make up his mind accordingly...

The story could have taken an altogether different turn. Perhaps, instead of a helpful or a noncommittal comment, the manager has another story – perhaps Swinger has left a trail of broken rafters and unpaid bills from Timbuktu to Tahiti, and he has been warned to be wary.

In this case the story would start to become unbalanced in the other direction. Now it is Swinger who deserves a comeback if he has one. At the very least, the facts being claimed by the manager need substantiation.

But once again, far from becoming less of a story, it is becoming the stuff of an interesting read. Things can't go on forever in this ping-pong fashion, of course, but wherever the story does end it should give all the relevant facts and treat both sides with equal fairness.

Other sins to avoid

Personal comment

It is sometimes very difficult to avoid expressing a personal opinion on some subjects being reported, or giving the words a 'slant' that reflects your point of view. This is especially so if your own standards of taste or behaviour are offended. Stick to the facts however. Any comment you make as a person can be interpreted as a comment made by the whole of your organisation, just as any comment given in a newspaper report gives the impression that it is the newspaper taking a stand (such cases of pontification or even implied approval or disapproval are known as 'editorialising'). Apart from anything else there can be legal implications to expressing opinions in print, no matter how harmless you may think them to be. Campaigning newspapers make their stands plain through special opinion columns written by the editor or a specialist leader-writer. To give a slant, personal, political or otherwise, to plain news, can only devalue the whole process of providing information, bringing into question its trustworthiness. The only exception to this comes when you are representing a political party, say, or a pressure group such as Friends of the Earth, when it can be stated that this is the organisation's definitive position on a particular subject, or when you have experts able to make informed comments.

Superlatives, tautology

Beware of further qualifying absolutes. A record fish is simply the biggest, not the biggest ever – you have added a word which means nothing at all. Tallest, latest, widest and other words expressing size, time or quantity ending in '-est' generally stand on their own. There are cases for breaking this rule but think carefully first. Be exceptionally wary of calling something 'unique' because things rarely are. Think before using 'massive' and 'huge' for similar reasons – 'big' will often do. And avoid tautology, saying the same thing over and over again in different words – e.g. *They got on the train in succession one after the other.* Always use short words in preference to longer ones where the meaning is the same, such as 'starts' rather than 'commences' and 'said' rather than 'commented'.

Ambiguity

Give everything you write at least one quick read to make sure nothing has a double meaning or an alternative interpretation that could bring ridicule upon you and by association your organisation (remember *'Eighth Army push bottles up Germans'*?). Rewrite until all meanings are plain.

Jargon and officialese

People in many trades and professions talk with one another using terms that can be totally incomprehensible to outsiders. Forms and documents from civil servants in particular have been noted for their contorted and labyrinthine construction, seemingly designed to confuse. Other members of society who should know better render tortuous accounts of events – a policeman, for example, told to leave out no details of attending the scene of a robbery, notes that he was 'proceeding along the High Street in a North-easterly Direction'. Actually, when I think of it, policemen should be arrested for some shortcomings. Our local force has started using 'mature male suspect' where 'man' would do, while teenagers are 'immature males or females between the ages of 12 and 17'.

When such offerings have become part of your story unscramble them. Make plain whatever is confusing, shed light where there is wordy murk. Above all use ordinary speech, as if you are talking to your neighbour over the garden fence.

Alas for the PR there are some areas where you will have to give in to your organisation, no matter how often you try to point out the error of their ways. One example that springs to mind is a social agency of Monmouthshire County Council which trendily calls itself 'adventa' with a small initial 'a', just as the better-known 'npower' starts with a small 'n'. Come on, school kids are being taught to give proper nouns a capital letter – so why are the press officers putting out Monmouthshire's news releases setting such a bad example, even when advent starts a sentence? Or npower's for that matter. Why are these organisations also giving sub editors the hassle of changing things back to Adventa? Would it make any difference to the organisation's work or image if it followed grammatical rules?

Car-maker SEAT's copywriting bods might seem similarly under the cosh. One interesting theory behind the use of all-capitals SEAT is that confusion might arise between the car and the things people sit on. In which case you might ask since when have seats (unless they be inside a car, train or other conveyance) gone from 0-60mph in eight seconds, or travelled 52 miles to the gallon? And when did they earn a proper noun's initial capital letter? It looks like hokum – but to be fair to the Spanish manufacturer the title is actually an acronym,

Sociedad Española de Automóviles de Turismo (Spanish Corporation of Tourism Cars), even though we pronounce it as a word. As if car-buyers don't already have enough trouble jargon-busting in motoring information with ABS, SIPS and the like!

General hints

Punctuation

The trend in most journalism these days is to use punctuation as lightly as possible so long as you can do so without destroying meaning or interpretation. Punctuation interrupts the 'flow' when someone is reading. If you look at the publications of earlier ages you will find that the much-punctuated type seems very stilted (they were sticklers for correctness!). Use as few marks as you can while striving for clarity – remember all punctuation has a part to play in making things comprehensible. Commas, for instance, come in pairs, defining clauses within a sentence, though the conjunctives 'and' and 'but' mean a second comma can be omitted. Used properly commas powerfully alter meaning as in:

> Mary said her mother had gone shopping.

compared with

> Mary, said her mother, had gone shopping.

Abbreviations

Strive for accuracy in all facts and figures, for instance making sure that lists of figures with a total do in fact work out to the correct conclusion. Likewise if you are unsure of anything don't compound the risk of upsetting someone – leave it out!

Apostrophes

Often misused. Apostrophes are not used with pronouns (ours, his, its, etc.) or with plural abbreviations (common errors where they should be left out are MP's, 1960's). The only circumstance where 'it's' is permissible is where it replaces 'it is'. The possessive of names ending in 's' do not need a further 's' after the apostrophe (e.g. St James' pyjamas were in the wash). Final apostrophes make nouns ending in 's' possessive, e.g. *The directors' absence was noted..*

Spelled numbers or figures?

It is general practice to spell out numbers from one to nine and give figures for any higher numbers, though once you reach a million you can start spelling again or mix both, as in *£8 million*. While the rest of the world makes a thousand million into a billion, the English have usually only accepted a million million as a billion. This is changing from general usage, but to avoid confusion give the actual figure and let someone else decide which billion is appropriate.

Avoid quirky little symbols

The use of tiny elevated (superior) 'th's as in 18th, elevated Centigrade Cs and percentage symbols all kick the inter-line spacing about in electronic DTP systems. They are worse for some fonts than for others and are best avoided either by spelling the abbreviation out (per cent, Centigrade) or using normal size letters (18th).

Lists, tables, results

In general lists of information which are to go into print are best submitted in run-on form:

> Longest runner bean: 1. D Hickstead (32 points), 2. P Marsh (28), 3. A Johnston (25).

A simple comma separates each listed item in this example but semicolons could be used.

Tabulated information is a little different since varied column widths rarely 'fit' submitted tables and most have to be retyped rather than cut and pasted. Best to avoid tabulation if you can.

Competition and sports reporting demands a little care over presenting team lists and results. Journals have individual ways of handling them, and if you submit a lot of material to one target it is wise to ask how they would like things presented.

Spelling

The use of the Oxford Dictionary is widespread in the British press.

Stay detached

Many members of the public regard the media as a mouthpiece to be used at their convenience and are affronted when wording is changed, or when somebody tries to tell them this or that simply cannot be used in such and such a way. It's forgivable of course for non-professionals to think that way, but not so for someone professing to be a press officer. However one sin regularly committed by those who should know better is slipping a royal 'we' into text, as in

> We would like to thank Marcia, Fred and Martin for providing the buns.

Who said that? The newspaper can't say it, now can it? Doesn't even know those people. Whoever sent this has forgotten they are trying to make what they have written as usable as possible and that means being as detached as if they were a reporter working for the journal or station concerned. Surely instead…

> The organisers said they wished to thank Marcia, Fred…

Remember you like that reporter are a professional observer, third person singular.

11

LAW AND COMMONSENSE

Libel, good practice, copyright

No press or PR officer should be unduly alarmed by the fact that there is a legal responsibility for accuracy and fairness on everybody who helps to put words into print. Although your work is more than likely to pass through an editor, you could ultimately be held accountable if people feel aggrieved or damaged by anything in your writing, since disseminating news is part of an act of publishing, i.e. making things known to the public at large through print or broadcasting. However, care over your copy avoids all the pitfalls. If you really are ever in doubt about material you have sent out, have a word with the editor and discuss any worries you have about legality, especially fears about libel or its spoken form, slander. Most publications and broadcasters will have a retained lawyer who is expert in libel legislation they can contact for advice over anything that seems risky. And while you may not be liable to pay damages personally if something goes wrong (sometimes huge amounts are awarded to aggrieved parties by courts), you will always thereafter be remembered as the person who dumped somebody in it.

Having said all that, such prosecutions are pretty rare and I can't recall a really significant one involving copy from a press officer!

As a general rule one should never present hearsay and gossip as copy, especially if you cannot check any of the facts surrounding the issue. By all means discuss current rumours and scuttlebutt with your target editor if you feel there is a need. But don't for instance repeat in print something you overhear in the canteen or pub as 'news' if you have not first checked if it bears scrutiny.

Be doubly wary of accepting information from people you suspect may have grudges to bear. They may be out to fix someone and you should not sign up to their agenda.

Although the average press or PR person is unlikely to set sail in these troubled legal waters there are a few points that should be borne in mind:

Libel

Defined in my dictionary as 'A published false statement, false accusation or malicious falsehood or misrepresentation in print, damaging to a person's reputation', libel is the most common action taken against the press. There is a great deal of room for varied interpretation of the above outline of the word depending sometimes on how much money the complainant can spend on a lawyer. It all comes down to how things are placed before the judge and whether or not he thinks a person's livelihood, reputation or standing have been damaged or 'defamed'. To give an example, one should be wary of stating that your current firm took over from a previously 'financially inept' management because a case could be argued that the forerunners were doing their best with the resources available to them and 'ineptitude' is an unfair description. Whenever you find yourself describing any sort of turnaround because of 'new' or 'better' management, alarm bells should be ringing.

Most actions taken under the libel laws are likely to be civil proceedings but following are some matters that attract criminal proceedings.

Contempt of court

Whenever charges likely to lead to a court case are brought against an individual or organisation, there should be no further discussion *whatsoever* of the circumstances of the case carried out in public outside the hearing until judgement has been made, because such discussion could influence the outcome of the action. The case is said to be *sub judice* until the matter is resolved. The bare facts of the names of people involved and the charges they face, as well as accurate reports of court proceedings, can be published (unless the magistrate, judge or recorder rules otherwise, or if they involve juveniles or sex and abuse victims who should be afforded anonymity – see below). From time to time press officers and PR people who have not had the benefit of journalism training are unaware of contempt laws when their organisation is involved in court proceedings and they should therefore be careful about what they report before the court is convened and while it is sitting.

Blasphemy

Another rarity but the legal requirement to avoid outraging Christian decency (other religions not being represented under this particular legislation) still stands in law.

Obscenity

Again, not a common cause of complaint these days but anyone involved in the 'adult goods' trade might keep a weather eye open for risky material in their handouts. The criterion is whether anyone who reads or sees the material in print will be 'depraved or corrupted' by its contents.

Incitement to religious or racial hatred

There are obvious dangers here in the wake of the 'war on terror' debate and legislation is in a state of flux. Stirring up hate, especially if it is likely to lead to violence, is certain to be prosecuted severely. Beware of inadvertently slighting racial or religious groups – this is where passions are easily inflamed and excuses, however good, are easily overlooked.

Juveniles, rape and abuse victims

The law tries to protect with anonymity those deemed to young (under 16) to fully responsible for their actions and victims of particular crimes who might suffer from being identified. Remember it is possible to identify people by 'jigsaw', i.e. mentioning a relationship or address which can be tied to them (see Code of Practice below) such as *'the accused is the victim's father, Fred Nasty'* or *'she lived in the same house as the defendant'*.

Code of Practice

A Code of Practice has been drawn up by the newspaper and periodical industry for its journalists which perhaps should also be read by press and PR officers likely to write on a regular basis for the press or broadcasting. It is enforced by the Press Complaints Commission (PCC).

It covers not just the legal aspect mentioned above but also gives valuable guidance to writers seeking to ask the crucial question referred to above: Is it fair?

Note that some of the clauses are marked with an asterisk* which denotes exceptions to the rules where publication can be deemed to be 'in the public interest'. Therein lies a lot of room for differences of opinion!

I have marked some passages particularly relevant to contributors in bold type, because the code actually acknowledges some material used in the media comes from contributed sources.

THE CODE

All members of the press have a duty to maintain the highest professional standards. This code sets the benchmark for those ethical standards, protecting both the rights of the individual and the public's right to know. It is the cornerstone of the system of self-regulation to which the industry has made a binding commitment.

It is essential that an agreed code be honoured not only to the letter but in the full spirit. It should not be interpreted so narrowly as to compromise its commitment to respect the rights of the individual, nor so broadly that it constitutes an unnecessary interference with freedom of expression or prevents publication in the public interest.

It is the responsibility of editors and publishers to implement the Code and they should all take care to ensure it is observed rigorously by all editorial staff **and external contributors, including non-journalists**, in printed and online versions of publications.

Editors should cooperate swiftly with the PCC in the resolution of complaints. Any publication judged to have breached the Code must print the adjudication in full and with due prominence, including headline reference to the PCC.

1. Accuracy

i) The Press must take care not to publish inaccurate, misleading or distorted information, including pictures.

ii) A significant inaccuracy, misleading statement or distortion once recognised must be corrected, promptly and with due prominence and – where appropriate – an apology published.

iii) The Press, whilst free to be partisan, must distinguish clearly between comment, conjecture and fact.

iv) A publication must report fairly and accurately the outcome of an action for defamation to which it has been a party, unless an agreed settlement states otherwise, or an agreed statement is published.

2. Opportunity to reply

A fair opportunity for reply to inaccuracies must be given when reasonably called for.

3.* Privacy

i) Everyone is entitled to respect for his or her private and family life, home, health and correspondence, including digital communications. Editors will be expected to justify intrusions into any individual's private life without consent.

ii) It is unacceptable to photograph individuals in private places without their consent.

N.B. Private places are public or private property where there is a reasonable expectation of privacy.

4.* Harassment

i) Journalists must not engage in intimidation, harassment or persistent pursuit.

ii) They must not persist in questioning, telephoning, pursuing or photographing individuals once asked to desist; nor remain on their property when asked to leave and must not follow them.

iii) Editors must ensure these principles are observed by those working for them **and take care not to use non-compliant material from other sources**.

5. Intrusion into grief or shock

In cases involving personal grief or shock, enquiries and approaches must be made with sympathy and discretion and publication handled sensitively. This should not restrict the right to report legal proceedings, such as inquests.

6.* Children

i) Young people should be free to complete their time at school without unnecessary intrusion.

ii) A child under 16 must not be interviewed or photographed on issues involving their own or another child's welfare unless a custodial parent or similarly responsible adult consents.

iii) Pupils must not be approached or photographed at school without the permission of the school authorities.

iv) Minors must not be paid for material involving children's welfare, nor parents or guardians for material about their children or wards, unless it is clearly in the child's interest.

v) Editors must not use the fame, notoriety or position of a parent or guardian as sole justification for publishing details of a child's private life.

7.* Children in sex cases

i) The press must not, even if legally free to do so, identify children under 16 who are victims or witnesses in cases involving sex offences.

ii) In any press report of a case involving a sex offence against a child

a) the child must not be identified
b) the adult may be identified
c) the word 'incest' must not be used where a child victim might be identified
d) care must be taken that nothing in the report implies the relationship between the accused and the child.

8.* Hospitals

i) Journalists must identify themselves and obtain permission from a responsible executive before entering non-public areas of hospitals or similar institutions to pursue enquiries.

ii) The restrictions on intruding into privacy are particularly relevant to enquiries about individuals in hospitals or similar institutions.

9.* Reporting of crime

i) Relatives or friends of persons convicted or accused of crime should not generally be identified without their consent, unless they are genuinely relevant to the story.

ii) Particular regard should be paid to the potentially vulnerable position of children who witness, or are victims of, crime. This should not restrict the right to report legal proceedings.

10.* Clandestine devices and subterfuge

i) The press must not seek to obtain or publish material acquired by using hidden cameras or clandestine listening devices; or by intercepting private or mobile telephone calls, messages or emails; or by the unauthorised removal of documents or photographs.

ii) Engaging in misrepresentations or subterfuge can generally be justified only in the public interest and then only when the material cannot be obtained by other means.

11. Victims of sexual assault

The press must not identify victims of sexual assault or publish material likely to contribute to that identification unless there is adequate justification and they are legally free to do so.

12. Discrimination

i) The press must avoid prejudicial or pejorative reference to an individual's race, colour, religion, sex, sexual orientation or any physical or mental illness or disability.

ii) Details of an individual's race, colour, religion, sexual orientation, physical or mental illness or disability must be avoided unless genuinely relevant to the story.

13. Financial journalism

i) Even if the law does not prohibit it, journalists must not use for their own profit financial information they receive in advance of its general publication, nor should they pass such information to others.

ii) They must not write about shares or securities in whose

performance they know that they or their close families have a significant financial interest without disclosing the interest to the editor or financial editor.

iii) They must not buy or sell, either directly or through nominees or agents, shares or securities about which they have written recently or about which they intend to write in the near future.

14. Confidential sources

Journalists have a moral obligation to protect confidential sources of information.

15. Witness payments in criminal trials

i) No payment or offer of payment to a witness – or any person who may reasonably be expected to be called as a witness – should be made in any case once proceedings are active as defined by the Contempt of Court Act 1981.

This prohibition lasts until the suspect has been freed unconditionally by police without charge or bail or the proceedings are otherwise discontinued; or has entered a guilty plea to the court; or in the event of a not guilty plea, the court has announced its verdict.

ii)* Where proceedings are not yet active but are likely and foreseeable, editors must not make or offer payment to any person who may reasonable be expected to be called as a witness, unless the information concerned ought demonstrably to be published in the public interest and there is an overriding need to make or promise payment for this to be done; and all reasonable steps have been taken to ensure no financial dealings influence the evidence those witnesses give. In no circumstances should such payment be conditional on the outcome of a trial.

iii)* Any payment or offer of payment made to a person later cited to give evidence in proceedings must be disclosed to the prosecution and defence. The witness must be advised of this requirement.

16.* Payment to criminals

i) Payment or offers of payment for stories, pictures or information, which seek to exploit a particular crime or to glorify or glamorise crime in general, must not be made directly or via agents to convicted or confessed criminals or to their associates – who may include family, friends and colleagues.

ii) Editors invoking the public interest to justify payment or offers would need to demonstrate that there was good reason to believe the public interest would be served. If, despite payment, no public interest emerged, then the material should not be published.

***The public interest**

There may be exceptions to the clauses marked* where they can be demonstrated to be in the public interest.

i) The public interest includes, but is not confined to:

a) detecting or exposing crime or serious impropriety
b) protecting public health and safety
c) preventing the public from being misled by an action or statement of an individual or organisation.

ii) There is a public interest in the freedom of expression itself.

iii) Whenever the public interest is invoked, the PCC will require editors to demonstrate fully how the public interest was served.

iv) The PCC will consider the extent to which material is already in the public domain, or will become so.

v) In cases involving children under 16, editors must demonstrate an exceptional public interest to override the normally paramount interest of the child.

Copyright

While copyright under English law means that the publication rights of written material belong to the individual who writes them (a right that can be sold, transferred or willed to another person or organisation), it is assumed naturally enough that material submitted by press officers and PRs is not only copyright free but also that nothing will be charged by the writer for re-using the material. However the occasion may well arise that the PR or press officer uses material from another source for their handout or press release, and care should be taken that nobody else's copyright is infringed by this – for instance an extract or quote from the work of a contemporary or a recent author. Up to 1996 copyright lasted for the life of the author plus 50 years, and in that year this was extended to life plus 70 years. Any such material used by a later writer should strictly speaking have their full approval and it is the later writer's duty to seek this and if necessary pay for it.

It is worth noting there is no copyright on ideas, just on the way they are expressed.

In some cases publications will offer to pay press officers for special duties like writing a match report, and it is useful to state that your material is released for first publication rights alone and you retain subsequent rights if you want to re-use your work elsewhere.

There is no room in this book to fully cover all aspects of copyright but if you want to look at the subject in depth there are extensive notes in publications like the *Writers' and Artists' Year Book*.

Copyright also extends to material used on websites and broadcast material.

A photographer is the first owner of the copyright of his or her photos *unless* there is some other agreement between the photographer and an employer (in the form of a contract of employment) or a person who commissions the photograph.

Data protection

Under the data Protection Act 1984 people must have access to personal data about them held in filing systems or on computer systems. This applies equally to an organisation's human resources details (a posh way of saying staff records), the PR, press officer or freelance correspondent's computers and newspapers and broadcasters' data files. People have the right to have data corrected if inaccurate, and a right to compensation for inaccuracy or unauthorised disclosures.

Official secrets

This is another area where there is much focus of attention because of the upsurge in terrorist activity, and care needs to be taken especially if the organisation you represent has any dealings with the armed forces.

There are six areas to avoid:

- Stories that might prejudice defence.
- Stories which prejudice security and intelligence.
- Stories that prejudice international relations.
- Information given in confidence by governments other than our own or by international organisations.
- Information useful to criminals.
- Information on Government telephone-tapping or interception of letters or other communications.

Section one of the Official Secrets Act 1911 remains in force. It is an arrestable offence to:

- Approach, inspect, pass over, be in the neighbourhood of or enter any prohibited place.
- Make any sketch, plan, model or note that might be or is intended to be useful to an enemy.
- Obtain, collect, record or communicate to any person any information that might be or is intended to be useful to an enemy.

Big brother could be watching!

12

IN THE PICTURE

In print journalism pictures are always welcome. It has often been said that a picture is worth a thousand words. Whether that's true or not, a picture of a product or event does help the reader's imagination along, while portraits with any story about an individual or a group of people immediately supply something that often has to be guessed. (*Gosh, you would never have thought a mass murderer looked like that, now would you?*) In most journalism the writer rarely goes beyond *'Petite blonde Mrs X said...'* or something similar, and in the world of petite blondes there are many variations, are there not? A picture defines exactly who you are talking about, facially at any rate!

Layout journalists love pictures to help make up and 'break up' their pages too (and with current print technology it is far easier to incorporate text and illustrations than it ever has been in the past). Ergo, any handout that handily comes with a picture, be it in hard copy print form, as a slide or as an electronic tif or jpg file, is very useful.

By far the most useful is the electronic file, providing it has sufficient 'pixels' to give good definition when the page is finally printed.

Time and again as an editor at the other end of the press handout line, the coalface, I (and a good many others) pick up a contribution that is crying out for illustration. Frequently editors have to send out their own photographers to accomplish this.

There are very few print organisations that still use film still cameras, though they do have their uses for really super quality studio work, design interiors, food photography and some landscape work. In the days when they were used for workaday purposes, the photographer first had to go out and take the shot than come back to a darkroom to develop and print it. This was only the start: the image was then transferred by an etching process to a light-sensitive metal plate (or several metal plates for a colour image). The processing leaves high points on the plate which either carry ink directly to the printing paper in a flatbed press, or transfer the image to a final curved plate in a traditional rotary press, or in modern litho printing transfers the ink to a rubber roller which lays the image down on the printing paper (offset litho).

Phew! Still, even that's not as bad as it used to be. Go back a few years more and the photographer, the man at the sharp end, had to take his wedding shots and scarper quickly before the oily black smuts from his magnesium flare started to settle on all those lovely white gowns!

The digital revolution

Digital pictures cut out an enormous amount of work for busy newspapers and magazines. It is not necessary to develop and print a hard copy, or scan anything, if attached files can be lifted directly from emails or transferred quickly from a camera memory card to the editorial computer system. The layout editor can adjust these files quickly and easily using programmes like Adobe Photoshop and drop them directly into pages constructed with desktop publishing (DTP) programmes such as Quark Express.

With this in mind it is recommended that every press officer, public relations officer or publicity officer has, and knows how to use, a decent digital camera which will plug into their own computer using a USB or some other form of connection. Preferably choose a well known make using memory cards which fit standard card-readers, just in case you have to download by other means. And pick one boasting high definition capabilities – almost daily they are getting better and better and cheaper and cheaper.

The power of the pixel

Definition in digital photography is determined by the number of pixels, or tiny dots, which make up an image. Here's web encyclopaedia Wikipedia's definition:

> Pixel: Short for ***Picture Element***, a pixel is a single point in a graphic image. Graphics monitors display pictures by dividing the display screen into thousands (or millions) of pixels, arranged in rows and columns. The pixels are so close together that they appear connected.
>
> The number of bits used to represent each pixel determines how many colours or shades of grey can be displayed. For example, in 8-bit colour mode, the colour monitor uses 8 bits for each pixel, making it possible to display 2 to the 8th power (256) different colours or shades of grey.
>
> On colour monitors, each pixel is actually composed of three dots – a red, a blue, and a green one. Ideally, the three dots should all converge at the same point, but all monitors have some convergence error that can make colour pixels appear fuzzy.
>
> The quality of a display system largely depends on its resolution, how many pixels it can display, and how many bits are used to represent each pixel. VGA systems display 640 by 480, or about 300,000 pixels. In contrast, SVGA systems display 800 by 600, or 480,000 pixels. True Colour systems use 24 bits per pixel, allowing them to display more than 16 million different colours.

Phwoar!

What matters most to a picture editor is the 'resolution' of the image, sometimes given with the camera's specifications as 'high', 'medium' or 'low' quality or resolution, or for example in a 6MB (number of recorded pixels) camera as a choice of 6MB, 3MB, 2MB and 1MB quality.

Sometimes picture editors use a dpi (dots per inch) method of defining digital picture quality, although Wikipedia scathingly points out that they frequently misuse this term to represent 'pixels per inch'.

> The number of pixels per inch in a computer display is sometimes specified as DPI as well. Usage of the DPI measurement in these cases is considered by some to be inaccurate and misleading, though the intended meaning is usually clear based on context.

> Another misuse results from an incomplete understanding of what the DPI measurement means. In order for any 'per inch' measurement to be meaningful, some number of inches must be specified. A digital image captured by a scanner or digital camera has no inherent 'DPI' resolution until it comes time to print the image (and even then, a more accurate measurement of image resolution is pixels per inch); for example, a 1,000x1,000-pixel image could be printed at 4x4 inches and 250 pixels per inch, or at 10x10 inches and 100 pixels per inch. Digital images contain some number of pixels; the size at which they are printed is relatively arbitrary. When someone asks for a '300 DPI image', they may be expecting an image with 300 pixels per inch of printed output; unless the size of the printed output is known beforehand, the measurement is meaningless.
>
> A more complete specification would include the desired print size in addition to the number of desired pixels per inch. A yet more complete specification would also include the DPI capability of the printer that will be used to print the image; if the printer is only capable of faithfully reproducing 100 pixels per inch, there is no reason to use a higher-resolution image.

But let's not worry too about all that, eh? The nitty-gritty is that newspaper editors are frequently happy with medium resolution photographs, rightly or wrongly designated as 200dpi (taking 15cm x 10cm as the standard size), while magazine picture editors are a bit more picky – The Radio Times, for example, and many other magazines ask for high resolution pictures only, or 300dpi and above. That would translate roughly to using the camera's 2MB capability for newspapers and 3MB for magazines, with occasional demands for higher quality for, say, a cover picture to be used as full A4 size.

But I digress, some of you might say in a wordy if not windy fashion. Just remember

- newspapers – medium resolution
- magazines – high resolution

and files of less than 1MB, unless they are to be used very small, say a 'thumbnail' head and shoulders shot, are practically useless to everyone who wants a decently faithful image to appear in print. Camera-phones generally only produce such small files. So do frames from video cameras. The examples you sometimes see in print have undergone huge amounts of enhancement or 'retouching'.

Know your limits

Unless your are an undiscovered David Bailey, simple shots like head-and shoulders portraits, and perhaps groups of two or more people, are the most useful digital photographs you can supply for print journalism. Within that range, however, there lie any number of situations, such as appointments, people moving on, presentations and retirement party groups (likewise groups at other company 'do's, such as product launches, or the unveiling of a new wing.)

It is unwise to attempt some things which are best left to the professional photographer:

- pictures of actual products where special lighting and all the paraphernalia of a photographic studio, not to mention special lenses, will turn a bar of soap into a 'must have' object
- sports pictures where action photography is a high art. (Try this yourself if you like – take your camera to a football or cricket match and take as many shots as you like. When you review them, count the times the ball has actually moved well out of shot by the time you pressed the shutter. Not surprisingly this can be quite a high figure.)

Portraits

All modern digital cameras (unless they are those ultra-mini spy cameras, or many phone-cameras) have a close-up/landscape toggle. You often don't want the formal stiffness of a passport photo, so try to get your subject to relax, perhaps cracking a joke while you take several shots from which you can choose the best.

Choose a neutral background – a plain wall for example. Outdoors when it is brightish and dry gives the best opportunity to find a spot that does not throw a shadow on the background. Indoors, you are more restricted and usually have to flash. Use a red-eye eliminator if you have one.

Groups

Group shots are best if everyone is informally arranged with the subject – say the boss presenting a bunch of flowers to a long-serving employee – at the centre or just off centre. Formal groups with everyone lined up, perhaps in two or more tiers, are known as 'firing squad' shots in the trade. Generally they are to be avoided but one exception is sporting teams, where such groupings are traditional before or after matches (maybe with the newly-won trophy at the players' feet or held aloft).

All photos: ground rules

You generally need the complicity of everyone you photograph if you are sending pictures out for publication. Apart from anything else, it is common courtesy to let them know the pictures are being submitted to a newspaper or magazine. Some people may have strong reasons for not wanting to appear in print. You might think you know everyone involved but what if one of them was a police informant living with a new identity to avoid felons finding and punishing him, perhaps even murdering him? More trouble occurs (and this is more common) when you photograph children, who could be relationship breakdown custody subjects, with a mum or dad trying to keep their location secret from a jealous or possibly vindictive ex-partner. Be aware of this when you are taking group shots. Ask first if there are objections, and keep whoever it is out of the picture whether or not they are prepared to tell you why they don't want the publicity.

Get all the names – full names!

Accompanying every picture should be caption material which explains the scene and its circumstances and names everyone involved. Assuming you have every subject's approval to take a picture it's a sin to then misspell their name, or make them semi-anonymous by using only their initials rather than a full first name plus family name. Take the time and trouble to make sure of the spelling, if necessary getting the subjects themselves to write their names down for you – especially useful if you have a picture of, say, a group of foreign dignitaries. If the people have titles, such as Mayor, include this before or after their name. The subjects of pictures are normally listed from left to right in captions (the viewer's left and right that is!). If you can, add the caption to the end of the attachment Word file or straightforward email story with which you send the picture (as a separate attachment file, preferably jpg).

Preparation and transmission

As mentioned above, mucking around with pictures using Photoshop or other programmes is best left to the journal that will be using them. Changes inevitably add to the overall size of the picture file, making it harder to handle and certainly hard to 'undo' as is often necessary. And if the actual image is tinkered with there can be legal considerations.

The most usual file type handled by the media is a jpg, and a phone call to the recipient will disclose the size and quality of files needed. For most press work a medium quality (medium resolution) jpg image is sufficient, sometimes specified as 200dpi 10x15cm file.

If higher resolutions are required you will usually be asked. Smaller files which 'look OK' will probably only be able to be used as very small reproductions indeed, because much definition is always lost in the printing process no matter how skilful the re-toucher's work.

Don't insert or embed your picture in a Word file or other text file because it takes time and work to untangle it. Send pictures and text separately. Similarly, try not to send more than two or three attachment pictures per email at a time. Big emails take more time to download and they are also likely to bounce back to you if a slot is not available on the recipient's server.

Email of course is not the only fruit. If you live close to your target you can call round in person with your picture on a disc or floppy, or you may have the picture downloaded directly from the camera if you have a USB connector or if the journal has a flash card reader.

Similarly, discs can be sent by post so long as they are reasonably well protected, although I would not advise sending a flash card because they are small and could be lost and replacements are far too expensive.

Film photographs

It is becoming rare these days to encounter a publisher who likes 'old fashioned' print or slide film – 35mm, two and a quarter square or whatever – but it can happen. However not all newspaper and magazine offices these days retain all the equipment necessary for processing and printing photographs. I make this point because it used to be a simple matter of sending off the whole unprocessed film to the editor in the certain knowledge they could handle all that business. Now, however, it would be best to send off a print – all of the recipients should at least have a scanner! It used to be the case too that it was more economical to buy 35mm cassette film as 12 frames rather than 24 or even 36, because individual jobs that have to be with the editor 'yesterday' might only amount to half a dozen or so shots. As I said, the use of film rather than digital photography is increasingly uncommon, but you might retain this information at the back of your mind in case it is needed.

If you are using film, make sure your caption information is included with the print or prints (usually OK to write on the back of the print with something that doesn't smudge – beware, common or garden biros do!).

Borrowed photographs

From time to time it is necessary to borrow pictures to accompany stories. It is wise to remember that such pictures are often cherished and absolutely irreplaceable if lost. A scanner is useful, so that you can make a copy of a print and hand the original back almost immediately, but this equipment is hard to justify when use is rare. If you do have to send somebody else's print out make sure it is well protected by card and that full return details are included – preferably a stamped envelope addressed back to the lender.

13

TRICKS OF THE TRADE

Competitions, giveaways, coupon promotions, sponsorship

Mostly this little book concentrates on the down-to-earth business of getting your news and information into print or on the airwaves by way of 'straight' press releases, but there are other ways of 'buying' space other than by paying up for advertising. The Press Officer should be aware of these 'tricks of the trade' which are useful ways of getting your information across, especially for new product launches. There are also useful ways of obtaining feedback on products or services with the cooperation of the press or commercial broadcasters, sometimes even public service broadcasters.

Competitions and giveaways, as well as coupon promotions, are all relatively cheap ways of approaching the advertising and hopefully resulting sale of goods and services, and details of these are given below together with another avenue that can be a little more expensive – sponsorship. I'd add 'charitable donations' to that last item. The big-prize survey can also be expensive but is a useful market research tool as well as a vehicle for putting your name and products in front of the public.

However it is always best to my mind to take the 'free' route first. One should never overlook the obvious human interest story, particularly one that can be geographically linked ('localised' is the trade term) to your target area, such as the visiting circus girl on the flying trapeze who is back in her home town for the first time since she ran away to start her career, or the rescue dog once scheduled to be put down but adopted by a loving local owner, and now (sponsored by Bow Wow dog food) in the finals of the top national agility trials. I could go on in this vein but you probably get the picture. Some such tales are good enough to gain national media exposure, but never turn away from the opportunity to exploit this area even if it does not look as if it will lead to sales: one is constantly surprised by the power of publicity of any kind. Obviously you should try to cram in as much product information as you can, but don't overdo it. The circus story ought at least to include a mention of the venue and dates and times of performances but even if it includes a nice picture of Fanny Fearless in full flight (cooperate here of course with the local press photographer) you cannot expect much more. Often though it will be enough to arouse considerable interest.

If you don't have a handy trapeze artiste or reformed canine menace it may be time to try another route.

Competitions and giveways

Both of these methods of 'buying space' without money changing hands have a similar approach, which first involves obtaining the cooperation of the journal or station concerned. So long as your offering to the public is a generous one, it is likely to be well received editorially – let's say, for example, 10 bars of new Blighton herbal soap with a pretty bath sponge or a loofah thrown in for the first 10 correct entries. The reader or listener likes to get things for free, and flagging up such a prize on the front page or 'pushing' it a bit over the air could win extra sales or new listeners/viewers. Prizes and offers also give overall added value to the media product, be it a publication or programme, reinforcing the bond with already-converted fans.

The difference between a 'competition' and a 'giveaway' is a fine one. Competitions usually take the form of a simple question with multi-choice answers, usually a, b, c, and with a few exceptions they are rarely taxing for the entrant. Often the correct answer is easily obtained from the information in the contest preamble, and a couple of spurious or obviously ridiculous items are thrown in to make it resemble a test of some kind. While this can seem faintly stupid there is a legal requirement on the media to make all items labelled 'competition' a game of skill rather than one of mere chance – the latter technically being gambling, for which a licence is required. Lip service is therefore paid to keep on the right side of the law.

By contrast a giveaway – say 10 bars of soap each to the first 10 postcards out of the hat or selected at random from email entries (no questions to answer in this case) – breaks none of the rules. At least, the principal has never been challenged...

Provided your prizes are acceptably valuable and you have agreed a format, you can send in promotional information to accompany the actual competition/giveaway.

Here is the standard promotional competition format you are most likely to encounter – notice it doesn't ramble on and on:

ENTER OUR GREAT BLIGHTON SOAP COMPETITION

Win a year's supply of herbal delights!

BLIGHTON soap has been a trusted household name for years but now the local firm has come up with a new herbal product which will make every bathtime a luxury health spa experience.

Blighton herbalists have searched the world for a range of health-giving herbal essences which they have incorporated in Herbal Spa, a luxuriously creamy soap which not only gently cleans but completely revitalises your skin, leaving you wonderfully refreshed.

From the Brazilian rainforest comes a delicate astringent drawn from the apple-like fruit of the Cashew tree (yes, the one the nuts come from), while from the Australian bush the oil of the Melaluca gently smoothes out wrinkles. Rhododendrons high in the Himalayas, their native home, provide a creamy essence that gently cleans as it soothes.

Blended with pure olive oil and delicately scented with lavender from sunny Provence, Herbal Spa is a completely new bath product everyone, young and old, will love – and it's available now at all chemists, stores and supermarkets.

Now you can enjoy this experience for free. (Publication's name) has teamed up with Blighton Soap to offer one of our readers the chance to win (grab?) a year's supply of Herbal Spa, with X runners up winning prizes of 10 bars each plus a luxury bath sponge.

All you have to do is answer the following question:

What is the native home of the Rhododendron?

a) Scotland
b) Himalayas
c) Snowdonia

> Send your answers to: Herbal Spa contest, Blighton Advertiser, 22 High Street, Blighton, Barts BT1 1AA to arrive no later than noon next Tuesday. Don't forget to add your name, address and a contact telephone number.
>
> Usual competition rules apply.

This is of course accompanied by a picture of the soap, and perhaps somebody stepping out of a bath (towel strategically placed) with a look on their face saying Herbal Spa is better than sex.

It is as well to note that competitions for prizes of alcoholic beverages or involving gambling cannot be entered by persons under 18 (the current GB qualifying drinking/gambling age), which is a fact that must be included in the write-up for such contests.

The inclusion of 'Usual competition rules apply' is another legality. Often these can go on forever and this form of words is acceptable so long as someone on the paper knows their competition rules! They will for instance include 'the editor's decision is final' and 'no correspondence may be entered into' (thereby avoiding tedious arguments with people who swear they have put their cross in exactly the right spot), 'cash alternatives will not be given' and so on. Happily, not an area which should unduly concern a Press Officer – but you will get credit for knowing the 'form'.

The astute will notice that not only do the names 'Blighton Soap' and 'Herbal Spa' crop up more than once, but a hell of a lot of product details are included despite the writing being fairly tight – including the fact that the soap is generally available (if otherwise this too could be mentioned, e.g. 'exclusively from Lloyds Chemists'). That's normal enough for this kind of promotion.

We have already looked earlier in the book at this product launch in terms of news value alone and have seen that in itself it warrants very little coverage (the facts that it is creating more jobs and raising the company's share profile proving a good deal more interesting than its bathroom attributes). And scant product information, let alone details of where it might be purchased, will have percolated through to the news pages without the 'hook' of a more interesting story to hang it on. Yet here in the competition, because of its 'value added' effect, a certain amount of free rein with product details and availability is allowed – a trade off, as it were, for giving the paper or broadcast more pull.

It has meant very little outlay for Blighton Soap in real terms yet the value to the punter is retail rather than wholesale or cost.

The product competition/giveaway is thus a valuable tool for a relatively 'hard' sell without paying out too much – and of course many more people take the trouble to read the competition than those who actually bother to enter. That's straightforward advertising unless I'm a monkey's uncle!

The competition and giveaway format can be applied in a wide variety of circumstances, offering services as well as goods, and is a great way of promoting events like concerts and big matches with free ticket prizes. While it might have no real appeal to the Women's Institute, it could well be used by the local football club as a promotion, either for tickets or shirts and other supporters' goods.

The Town Council, again, might view it as a vehicle with little use but any public utility, in what is a very competitive market, could get something going in order to promote its services and earn new customers – offering a quarter's free bills, perhaps, or even a cash prize to carry the organisation's selling points. Our example museum uses it often to offer free entry to some of its regular staged events throughout the year.

Market research/survey prize draws

A handout stating that such and such a firm is conducting a study into the appeal of its product and would be grateful if readers would help is likely to go straight on the editor's spike. Why should they do your job for you? If you want to find out this information, go and ask it. Get a market research firm to do it for you if you like, but don't expect any response from the media. What's in it for them? Not extra readership or sales. It would just be wasted space.

Look, pay for a whopping great advert if you like, asking for public response. I doubt that would be money well spent – you'll be lucky to get a handful of replies, if any.

But what if you were to offer a draw with a cash prize (or a holiday or a car) to everyone who submits a completed tick-box questionnaire? Now that's a different story.

Now the situation is very much the same as its is for the competition or giveaway described above: the readers get a tempting offer, you get your information, and the editor gives his paper or programme more pull. Once again everyone's a winner – except perhaps the 100,000 people whose submissions weren't the first out of the hat!

Once again, it's necessary to have the complete cooperation of the publication or programme chief to make these arrangements – and sometimes journals like the daily and Sunday papers canvass surveys off their own bat with the cooperation of business sponsors who put up a big prize array in return for the sort of multi-question survey which can help them plan their business strategies for some time ahead.

Travel surveys are a good example. If you work for firms where this sort of survey is appropriate for your needs it might pay you get in touch with the publication or programme concerned. You may not be able to contribute much from your organisation but in the case of travel surveys the prize 'pot' from several small organisations and a few big players soon grows to a very healthy size, and the surveys consequently attract a huge response.

Coupon and serial promotions

Yet another way to buy 'free' product promotion is the coupon approach, which has the added advantage of spreading the word over longer periods of time. Readers (and of course it has to be readers because you just can't get coupons transmitted over the airwaves unless you work aboard the Starship Enterprise) are asked to collect a certain number of coupons in order to claim a free product, say a hamburger. It's another one the editors like, because it does give them a front page 'hook'. It can also cost you very little in goods or services.

I'd include with this any offer stating 'entry free to anyone showing this copy of the newspaper' or 'cut out this advert and bring it along for 20 per cent discount', but beware the serial photocopiers if your offer is a good one – the best idea is to bar photocopies altogether, or stipulate 'offer limited to one per person'.

Sponsorship

Like prize draws in return for product feedback, sponsorship and gifting are more expensive ways of getting information into print or on the air. However they can be extremely effective. Sponsoring, say, a new football strip for the local football club – seniors or juniors – is not only worth a team photo of the lads or lasses in their new kit, but whenever pictures are taken of them in action on the field, your name should stand out on the chest (or breast) of every player in focus. Junior football teams are often very needy and these 'gifts' are very welcome. However, it is best to suggest that contacts with the media are made via the club concerned rather than coming directly from you. However, it is perfectly in order for sponsors to be photographed with the receiving team – your boss might like to be the firm's token representative for the warm glow this sort of publicity stunt involves.

Gifting is very similar – a 'gratis' cheque for £100, £200, whatever towards the local hospice or national funds like Children in Need is worth a picture of the handover (with one of those giant cheques of course) with a little caption story – for example, 'Ken Jones, mayor of Blighton, hands over £150 surplus from last year's Christmas lights fund to Helen Masters of the Victoria Rooms OAP Lunch Club'. Lucky Ken hasn't even had to fork out himself for that one, and neither can anyone claim it's coming out of the council tax! In this instance and others like it, it is absolutely fine for you to alert the press to presentations or even contribute the picture and caption information yourself.

Briefly, while on this subject, it is worthwhile for every press and PR officer to foster workforce participation in charitable campaigns such as Children in Need – it's good for internal relations as well as for bringing the company name into any publicity these activities generate.

Pitching promotions

In all promotional areas other than sponsorship/gifting it is vital to pitch your initial ideas directly to your media targets rather than going to the trouble of putting everything together first. Rejection can hurt more if you've put time and effort into the project. The idea needs to lodge with someone who not only has the authority to carry the thing through, but also someone you can cooperate with right through to its completion. Get a name, latch on to them!

Matters that need to be agreed for, say, a newspaper competition are the nature and value of the prize or giveaway item/service, whether or not you or the newspaper (usually the latter) will judge the entries, and who will hold and distribute the prizes – you or them.

If you do take on the judging you will see for yourself how popular or otherwise the competition has been, but beware there may be cost involved if the responses are numerous and require individual scrutiny. If you end up making the draw it is wise to shred all unsuccessful entries. If any are ever found blowing around the streets from a burst bin bag, the people who took the trouble to send them in can get quite upset.

As well as agreeing on these matters you should ask roughly how many words are required and provide product pictures and any other relevant images.

I would not bother to do more than label the bare facts by way of a headline – Soap offer from Blighton – leaving the paper's creative staff to 'dress up' the competition in their particular style. However I might ask to see how they have treated it, if possible, before it goes to press. If they have made any mistakes that you could have corrected, it will be on your head!

Despatch prizes promptly – thwarted gratification is another area where people can get very annoyed. If the prize is particularly good or valuable you might suggest that the paper carries a picture of the presentation, but use your judgement before insisting on this point. Normally just a paragraph to say who has won what is included by the paper as a matter of course just to show that people do actually win their (your) competitions.

If you are pleased with the result, always say so, perhaps thanking the contact individual and journal concerned. You may want to repeat the exercise some time!

14

GOING TO AIR

Liaising with broadcast journalists on the simple 'handout' level is little different from handling the print media. The editorial set-ups are very similar and both kinds of organisation have the same anxieties about looming deadlines. It's just that instead of words being transformed into column inches in print, in this case they represent seconds and minutes of the airtime they occupy. And, like print, this can be estimated with a fair degree of accuracy and contributions can be edited to fit a particular number of seconds.

The difference comes when you are asked to take a 'live' role in the proceedings by making a statement or comment on your news contribution. This can either be in a studio or on location – normally your workplace or the workplace you represent.

In the studio

In some ways, until you get used to the situation, working in a studio can be very nerve-wracking. In spite of your interviewer/presenter's efforts to put you at ease – and they will do their best here – the situation is entirely artificial for the 'conversational' effect they will try to create. In the radio studio, for example, there's a microphone in front of you (or swinging your way on a flexible arm) whenever it is your turn to speak, and in the TV studio there's the addition of the unwinking eye of the camera, or perhaps more than one. Each of these 'third parties' in your conversation could represent thousands of listening/viewing people! Crumbs!

The trick, you realise after a while, is to ignore these distractions as if they were not there, and concentrate instead on the person you are talking to – and of course what you are saying. It is important to remember that you are surrounded by professionals who take care of everything from the levels of sound to the picture they are creating. There is no need to play to the microphone, leaning closer to emphasise a point, or keep moving yourself to give the camera what you think is a good angle (showing your best side, of course!).

The studio staff for their part should be doing everything in their powers to make you feel comfortable and appear natural, and in the case of TV this can mean makeup attention to ensure you are not a sweating nervous wreck, even if that is the way you imagine you are coming over.

Behave as naturally as possible. Behave as if you were talking to a friend across a pub table, only in this case think just a little before you speak! And don't 'talk posh' just because you think it's appropriate in the situation. Don't forget to breathe naturally between statements. Relax.

You should soon get the hang of it.

Now you can if you wish (and if you have time) practice what you are going to say before you attend the studio, and I know some people read out statements to a tape recorder and play them back to see what they sound like. To my mind that encourages talking unnecessarily slowly or clearly and it can sound quite artificial. It also shows you up when you are asked something unexpected, off the cuff, and you respond in a totally different voice. I find it better just to memorise the main points and work with the interrogator – it comes out better in the end. It is quite a good idea, however, to write a little summary of what you want to get across on, say, a filing card, so that you can give it a quick scan before the microphone or camera heads your way. And if you have somebody else's quote to deliver 'on camera' it is quite in order to have it written out, and to read from your 'crib' on air. And if you can't answer a question or it would be diplomatic from your point of view to avoid an answer (if your job's on the line for example!) just say you are unable to answer without more information – even if you are in a corner where a simple 'yes' or 'no' is all that is required. Stick to your guns.

On location

I spent some of the time I was living in Melbourne, Australia, trying to get recordings of the city's ubiquitous blackbirds, first exported to the country by homesick Brits in the late 1800s. I wanted to send them back to Britain for possible use as a 'guess where this was recorded' item in a radio wildlife programme. Try as I might, although this meant rising at the crack of dawn on several mornings, I could not eliminate background urban noises – cars starting up, garage doors slamming, creaking gate hinges, the distant rattle of a tram, the fluted notes of nearby Australian magpies. I must have been entirely green at the time because I did not take into consideration that the background noises – particularly the rattling tram and the magpies – gave my recordings a sense of place and something broadcast journalists call 'colour'.

Brought up in a print tradition and therefore not being sound and vision oriented, I am afraid I had not learned my lesson even later on and in this country when I remarked to the local BBC reporter out on the same job I was covering 'I expect you have an awful lot of trouble cutting out the background racket' which in this case was a busy main road above which an aggrieved homeowner who was about to be evicted under a compulsory purchase order was carrying out a rooftop protest ('I won't come down until I get justice,' he was shouting).

The radio reporter looked very surprised. 'What?' he said, 'We like background noise. The more the better. How else do people know where we are?'

I offer my flash of revelation, along with my blushes, as a helpful hint to anyone who is going to be interviewed or make a statement in situ: for radio places, try to choose a spot that will 'illustrate' where you are with a sound – for example the background factory noise of a carpet loom – while for TV you might choose a location representative of your firm's activities or its products (but *not* overt advertising, particularly where the BBC is concerned!).

Thus for an interview about a football club's prospects, you might arrange a background of some of the players in training, while in a factory you might like to be interviewed on, say, a gallery above the shop floor unless the racket is unbearable. Very rarely is the boardroom a suitable interview location, since all boardrooms seem to look so much the same.

Hostile interviews

Thankfully it is rare to find yourself in a hostile interview situation but if you ever are under such fire – the firm has just announced mass redundancies and people are baying for blood, for example, or its toxic waste has just poisoned 90 miles of prime salmon fishing – in these cases it is important most of all to keep your cool and beware of letting yourself be goaded into saying something that had not been agreed with your manager or board. You may feel as if you are about to be lynched but in a civilised world the messenger is rarely shot. If asked to toe a line, then toe that line. As I have already stated, there are ways of averting probing questions, and they all mean much the same thing, which is, 'get off my back'. They include:

- *I do not have that information at the moment*
- *We cannot comment on that at this time*
- *We are addressing the problem*
- *When there is something to say we will make a further statement*
- *I'm afraid that is all we have to say for the time being*

On delivering such a line gather all your papers with a businesslike rustle, stuff them into your briefcase and beat a smart retreat – don't hang about for people to keep niggling. It is in the nature of all journalists to keep digging but they do respect a professional 'bugger off' when they see (or hear) one. And on TV clamming up makes a dramatic little windup scene. See also the Bad News Day chapter.

15

BAD NEWS DAY

The sales figures are disastrous, the shares are in freefall. At this very moment the MD and the chief accountant are climbing the stairs to the roof where they plan to hold hands and jump. When the bad news hits the streets it will make matters much worse. Is there anything that can save the day?

Divine intervention, perhaps. Or, just possibly, a well managed, well crafted press statement. One that makes people think there's life in the old firm yet. If they can just hang on there's light at the end of the tunnel. That black cloud looming over the suicidal execs on the roof may well have a silver lining...

I'm not saying it is easy to spread a little cheer when all about is doom and gloom, but it can be done. It does of course require the cooperation of those around you, particularly the boss. If he or she can't be found at this point, run to the bank with any company pay cheques you have not yet cashed, then head for the Jobcentre with everybody else. Let me make it clear that what I am particularly not saying is that you should help to buy the management time to make good their escape before angry creditors and an angrier workforce catch up with them – there has to actually be some sort of rescue strategy on the table, some shred of optimism, or whatever words you use will be condemned as weasel words.

First, recognise that all matters are delicate when the chips are down. The wrong message will obviously make matters worse, as I have already suggested, while an over-optimistic view of the situation will probably be laughed at by all concerned. But more than anyone else you should be the best person to steady everyone's nerves. Why? Because you have a way with words...

I know disaster comes in many forms (not always in threes!) and what follows may not be applicable to every situation. However you can hopefully find something in the suggestions below that will help.

The biggest threat, the thing that is most likely to upset the whole apple-cart, is the anger that is bound to be manifest whichever way you look – the workforce and their unions will be angry about job losses, creditors and shareholders will be angry about losing their money, and the management itself may well be angry about finding themselves in such a pickle – after all only out-and-out crooks willingly steer the ship on the rocks so that they can take the pickings. Chances are that if things have gone wrong through ineptitude, through misreading markets, through a million and one foreseeable and not so foreseeable causes, the boss and probably the whole board will feel proper charlies. Anger on everyone's part is a natural reaction but it should be channelled into a force for cooperation rather than a force for wreaking even more havoc.

Your first task is to explain to all concerned that the unfocussed anger coming from all quarters has never won the day, and then say in a clear voice in any little island of peace you can create that you could offer a few suggestions *provided* the firm or organisation has even a remote chance of surviving as a leaner/smaller/more careful/more productive enterprise.

When this attracts everyone's attention, as it should, explain that positive statements to the outside world are paramount if recovery is to succeed, and hit them with this fact: it ain't what you say, it's the way that you say it. To which you might add that some of the best companies/organisations in the world have hit bad times, some of them recovering completely from situations worse that your own.

By now your peaceful island should start to acquire some nice little sandy reed-fringed bays where it may be possible to glimpse calm waters beyond! Keep going while the sweetening breeze is still blowing in your favour.

First, everyone should realise what's done is done. They feel as if they have had a bucket of ice-cold water thrown over them while they were lazing happily in bed on Sunday morning, but now there's no changing the facts. All that can be done is to get up and get on with washing the sheets, and drying the mattress. The fairies won't do it while you shiver and mutter and fume about it. Take some positive steps (that word *positive* again).

The internal battles are usually the hardest ones to overcome, and a lot of this is down to someone (or many) having to swallow their pride. If culpability for the situation exists it is always best to come clean at the very least to the workforce (not that workforces themselves are immune from dumping organisations in grief). It's the point where most people feel like withdrawing into their shells but exactly the opposite is what should be happening. It's all a matter of being positive rather than negative. And admitting culpability is not in itself negative. If anything, it earns respect. It's also like taking a deep breath and getting ready to go back into the fray.

By now people should be starting to ask you exactly what your suggestions are other than just being nice to each other. Here's where you say it is critical for everyone to present a positive picture to the outside world that will restore your organisation's standing (or avoid losing it in the first place).

There's usually no point in denying that problems exist. You'll fool nobody in a world where the media has sniffer dogs out constantly searching for trouble of any kind. The more you try to gloss over relevant facts the harder investigative journalists will work to get to the truth, and assuredly the truth will out. Nor do most organisations have the luxury of waiting until some other major national or world disaster presents itself as an opportunity to 'bury bad news' (oh how a certain person wishes she had never considered using those words!).

Rest assured there is a positive form of words for almost every shaky situation that can befall you.

Job losses

If jobs are to go it is no use denying the fact either to the workforce and their unions or to the press. Denial does nobody any favours. Remember always that the company (and you) would not willingly be in this situation. The anger we talked of above will quite probably lead to blame being apportioned somewhere. The witch-hunt is a natural reaction. But press officers cannot let anything like that get to them, no matter how much ear-bashing they get. Keep emphasising the fact that any corporate failure is just what it says on the tin – whether they like it or not, everyone has a hand in what goes down. What might genuinely cause grievance, the inequalities that can be seen in the relative wealth of the bosses and the lowly workers if the whole enterprise folds (*'You can bet your bottom dollar Sir Nigel's come out of it OK'*), is usually nothing to do with the situation itself, unless some real injustice has been perpetrated, such as the pension fund being raided. We all work in a capitalist environment, and short of bloody revolution that's not going to change in the foreseeable future.

To the job losses then. You regret them or rather the management does, it goes without saying – only in this instance you make a point of saying so loud and clear. The other phrases and 'forms of words' which will probably be of use to you are:

- *'The company is doing all it can to find its (valued) workforce other jobs/positions within/outside the firm.'*
- *'The company hopes most of the losses will come through natural wastage as employees leave or retire'*
- *'The company hopes the situation will be short-lived and it will be able to re-employ several of the lost workers.'*
- *'The company is working with the workforce/unions on an acceptable redundancy package.'*
- *'The company has adhered strictly to current redundancy rules and regulations.'*
- *'The company has consulted its workforce at all stages of negotiations.'*

And finally:

- *'The company recognises the hardship its decision may cause the workers (the suppliers, the local community) and is doing everything in its power to help everyone concerned.'*

Now I won't pretend any of the above won't be greeted with some scepticism by the press, who recognise a good get-out clause when they see one, but they will be bound to use whatever statement you use in this situation.

And that, in the end, is what counts in print or on airtime – the image of a good employer duly concerned about the fate of the people who have been working for him. If you say nothing, you can bet the other 'side', the aggrieved workers, will say plenty. Remember 'balance'? The organisation which makes 'no comment' is an organisation condemned!

Forms of words for concurrent or other situations? Okay...

Sales slump

- *'The company hopes it will be able to weather the downturn and come back to the market with renewed vigour.'*
- *'The company is taking a long look at its product/services range and exploring new avenues/markets for sales.'*
- *'The company says it is hopeful of full recovery when its planned new product range comes on stream.'*
- *'The company says the severity of the downturn had taken everybody by surprise and they have learned lessons which will be valuable in the future.'*

And so on and so on ... I am sure you get the idea.

Financial crash

- *'The company is restructuring its finances.'*
- *'The company is hopeful of attracting new investment.'*
- *'Even at this late stage there are hopeful signs...'*

Finally, recite to yourself Kipling's 'If'. It's a wonderful tonic even if you do feel like the proverbial snowball in hell!

16

GOOD NEWS DAY

You've won the cup. A new manufacturing process has enabled you to slash your prices. Process output has beaten all records. Sales figures have gone through the roof. Profits have doubled, nay trebled. You've taken over the rival firm. Everything in the garden is rosy, and it's good news all round – for the managers, the workers, their families, the community round about, and certainly for the readers of the local papers, perhaps the nationals too, and the same goes for the listeners and viewers of radio and TV stations.

Of course you want to shout this from the rooftops. For one thing, good news is in short supply – it's a world where disaster more often than not occupies the headlines. No editor worth his salt would turn his back on a counterpoint to all that flood, fire, pestilence and plague – carry too much gloom and you run the risk of alienating readers/listeners/watchers wholesale.

For another, good news is a real chance to give your organisation some really positive publicity, and that can have a real influence on sales or support. It's also a wonderful morale booster for the rest of the workforce, something that directly affects productivity.

Here's a real chance to put on a big campaign, so don't mess about with half measures or a trickle of news. Instead, aim to get a notice in as many publications and on as many TV and radio stations as you can. Consult your contacts book, plunge in.

Make hay while the sun shines

Unlike disaster, success is often short lived. By its very nature something comes along to detract from it, even negate it, unless by some miracle something even more successful comes along to swamp it. But hey, isn't the result then the same, putting the initial bit of good news in the shade? Remember tomorrow is another day and it will very likely present a completely different set of scenarios. Sufficient unto the day is the evil thereof.

Act quickly as you can. Pull out all the stops, all the tricks you can muster, and call in all the favours.

If your operations are generally low key in the scheme of things, like having to cope with an ancient desktop computer and no means of taking pictures, you would be justified in asking for extra assistance at a time like this – maybe the help of the IT department to disseminate your material, and perhaps a by-your-leave to call in a local freelance photographer to take some pictures to accompany your press releases.

Get pictures, above all, that reflect corporate happiness allied if possible to the agent which created the excitement – the beaming boss with the firm's latest model washing machine, your newly-signed striker with an ear-to-ear grin twirling a football on his fingertip. Have a variety of pictures taken so that no two targets, at least not those known to be close rivals, have the same picture – and most important in this instance let them know that particular shot is exclusively theirs. Invite the closest news organisations in geographical terms to come and take their own photographs, write or record their own reports from the facts you can supply them with.

It might well pay to first 'flash' the good news around all your targets and let them know a full release is being crafted and will be with them shortly – that at least will allow those right up against their deadlines to slip in a 'breaking news' paragraph somewhere.

Smaller miracles

Corporate successes are not the only bits of good news occurring in daily life – in a workforce, as in any group of people, there are triumphs as well as disasters, and if reported properly, the triumphs can 'rub off' on the image of your firm or organisation. Births and marriages are particularly fertile ground, especially exceptional events like the birth of triplets, or the boy-meets-girl wedding story of the couple who first met in the welding department (what a picture opportunity – sparks flying!). As well as this there may be employees who have served the organisation for a long time, or perhaps several generations of a particular family who all work for the same company; there may be employees or groups of employees who win the Lottery and other major prizes and stay (or go), and there may bee employees who undertake feats such as skydiving to support a charity or swimming backstroke across the Channel for the same worthy ends. All are worth some 'good news' treatment that gives your organisation at the very least a namecheck and at best a picture in words or as an image that shows it in a good people-oriented light.

17

ADVANCED TRICKS

How to handle your media

Listen, I don't want you to run away with the idea that this is all about trickery or has anything at all that creaky about it – far from it. All I want you to realise is that this is how the media world works and how you can often turn some of these facts to your advantage.

Ordinarily a lot of press officers don't even think about the following points simply because it has just not crossed their minds that every media 'customer' has unique characteristics. Weekly, daily (free or paid for), morning regional papers, national papers, magazines specialist and general, newsletters, commercial and public (BBC) radio and television might as well be a flock of sheep to them for all the differences they can see between them. And that is the way they are treated when it comes to disseminating press releases – everybody gets exactly the same item, words and, in the case of print outlets, pictures, at virtually the same time. That's vastly more easy now too, with the internet – you can send the same communication to a whole raft of recipients by simply pressing one button.

In fact they are all vastly different animals, with unique characteristics that the astute press officer can exploit, for want of a better word. And another key point to bear in mind is that they are all in competition with one another, even those within the same 'stable' or parent company. If you ever feel you haven't heard a good groan for a long time and would like to hear one, phone up any editor of any publication you like and say you have a good story which the editor of the paper/station down the road has already agreed to take!

Consider also the following facts which I have attributed to a range of fictional media not unlike the situation in most parts of Britain – I can certainly show you places where it is very similar, right down to the figures quoted. I'll summarise what it all means to you at the end. We'll start with circulation (or listener/viewer figures), adding deadlines and geographical range. And let's view it all from the perspective of the press officer working for a small but reasonably successful company in District X, a small but far from sleepy corner of what an American might call 'one of your British shires'. From what I have seen the US media make-up is not vastly different. In this lies information that can not only help you to decide what you send out, but who you send it to and even when to send it to the best advantage.

The media food chain

A **Free district weekly**, circulation 50,000 (audited), deadline noon Tuesday, range 30 miles radius of HQ.

B **Paid-for district weekly**, 12,000 (declared), deadline 5pm Wednesday, range as 'free'.

C **Evening paper** for nearby large town with district edition, 4,000 for edition 35,000 overall, 4 deadlines daily but only the earliest for our district, range as above for district but will include 'important' news across all editions with a range of perhaps 60 miles from base.

D **Commercial local radio station** in town, listeners in low hundreds in daytime and evening depending on other attractions but perhaps a thousand or so in 'drive time' to and from work, range to county boundaries but absent in 'blind' radio spots.

E **Local BBC station** (largely as above).

F **Regional morning paper** based in county town, circulation perhaps 4,000 for our district on a good day, deadline round 7pm daily, range across county and beyond in some spots.

G **National magazines**, general and specialist (deadlines and ranges N/A).

H The **national press, national radio** and **TV** (commercial and BBC). The domestic news deadlines are much the same as for the regional morning paper, even for 24-hour rolling news broadcasts, since most of Britain literally goes to sleep in terms of news for a great deal of the night – most 'action' has died down, there are no courts sitting, even the MPs and Peers have stopped barracking each other across their respective debating tables. You'd be mad to keep staff on at such a time so there's usually some poor mug on the 'dead man's shift' wrestling with tomorrow's crossword and fighting off the impulse to go and have a peek in the drawer where the next day's solutions are kept.

Moving on to what this all implies I would like to explain a few other facts about some of these media outlets that have some bearing on how you might use them.

The free weekly for a start. What a whopping circulation – it's clear to see that if you want something noticed locally, this is the place to target! Why does it have a big circulation? Because it is shoved through people's letterboxes whether they want it or not. And it is massively full of advertising, because advertising is what pays the proprietor enough cash to have it distributed, pay his staff and leave a reasonable profit margin. Now it may come as a shock to many, but all print journalism unless it is very specialist stuff for societies and the like is about making money, with the dissemination of news and information, while important, secondary to profit. If the print bills and payroll cannot be met from the combination of cover sales and advertising (or advertising alone in the case of frees), the publication folds. But back to our 'free' – how much notice is taken of the news content by the average recipient is often a matter of how good it is, and there are some very good examples where news gathering is taken seriously. Conversely there are more than a few 'turkeys' where after a glance over the ads the thing goes straight in the reader's bin. And if you study frees over a period of time you might notice something else – the amount of editorial space from week to week is either a famine or a feast. Sometimes there's barely room for a bit of news on the front with odds and ends squeezed in between the ads inside, while next week there may well be page after page of editorial. It is all down, of course, to the fact that you cannot add a page at a time to a newspaper because the configurations of paper-folding, printing and trimming mean that for the most part any pagination increases have to go up in sections of eight pages at a time. If the advertising goes even marginally over 56 pages, for example, a 64-pager will have to be printed with the bulk of eight more pages going to editorial to fill up.

All of this often has to be put together at the very last minute, usually involving quite a small editorial cast – journalists in this case coming a poor second to advertising sales staff on the payroll. Consequences for the press officer? Yes. Your contribution, regardless of how good it is, might get a good show, might get a poor show, or might not get included at all if it's a bad week space-wise. If it does all right however it gets an audited circulation which probably tops the combined readership/listening and viewing figures of all the other media serving the district.

We can't leave the 'free' without noticing that its deadline is Tuesday lunchtime compared to its 'rival' paid-for weekly's deadline the next evening. Keep that in mind.

So what can the 'paid for' do for you? Let's first look at a few things that are almost certainly not obvious, the first of these being that it is owned by the same large newspaper group which owns the evening paper in the nearby town. While it has an old and distinguished district name it has been bought from the original independent owners in the not too distant past and is now being supported in its efforts to knock the 'free' off its pedestal and, at the same time, keep any other piratical publications out of the district (a 'spoiler', this is called in the trade). It therefore has the rather privileged position of being able to plough most of its advertising revenue back into making a good-looking editorial product with a guaranteed regular large amount of editorial space. Again, can you use this? Yes. Especially if you have a good but 'soft' story that will look good pictorially. With space and a bigger editorial staff they will be able to make the most of what you have sent them (but don't forget here that point about being in competition with publications in the same stable).

Remember those deadlines though? I know I have advised

strongly on getting urgent news out as far and as fast as you can, but material that can be held for its most opportune release date should probably in this instance be tendered first to the free on the grounds that it will enjoy the widest possible coverage.

Why not offer the same stuff to both ahead of both deadlines? Because they will assume the story is shared and this will detract from the prominence they feel able to afford it. Why not offer it to both after the free's deadline but before the paid-for goes to the press? Fine if you want it to have a better show, because the paid for will realise the free now has to wait a whole week before it can run the story (and the free may not run it at all in preference to carrying 'old' news that has already been broken).

Before leaving the two weeklies behind, it is worth pondering why the paid-for has not exceeded its rival in circulation (a factor which directly affects its appeal to advertisers and also the amounts it charges for advertising space). It is after all a showier 'product' than the free. The answer is, of course, that the paid-for's circulation is actually a reasonably natural level for a weekly newspaper in our district. And the trend for most of the provincial press circulation figures in Britain is moving steadily downwards in the face of factors such as new media and a barrage of information from other sources like TV. Unless our paid-for declares itself 'free' and challenges the rival by adopting the same distribution methods, it may well be 'stuck' with its present circulation level. If it moves in the 'free' direction – and the city edition of the Manchester Evening News has started to do just this – it begins to need to adopt the same market economics as a 'free' and the pressures on editorial space already mentioned. Greater challenges are in fact looming for the provincial press, with big news websites in Los Angeles and San Francisco already offering free classified advertising listings, until now a revenue mainstay of local papers. (*'What California is today, the rest shall be tomorrow.'*)

When you learn about these things you are halfway towards making the best of the media. Keep an eye on these things and examine them for the benefits or disadvantages they might bring you. For any press officer the media pages of papers like the Guardian are almost compulsory reading.

Now to the town evening paper with its district edition. While in the case I have given it is 'in bed' with the weekly district paid-for, this situation is by no means general, with some successful paid-for weeklies remaining independent. Be that as it may, in this instance the evening could share all its information with the paid-for but chooses instead to maintain its editorial independence for the sake of keeping its district edition going – to this end it will try to dig out stories the weeklies have not discovered. But with this move up the food chain there is another factor in play – monitoring. The evening will notice and follow up on its own behalf any of the weeklies' stories it believes will have appeal to its wider all-editions readership.

On the face of it this means you might reasonably expect a release sent to either of the weeklies would, by osmosis, find its way into the evening too (and indeed further on up the chain, but more of this later). All right, that's a valid assumption – but think about it first: it may not have the immediacy you need, if you see what I mean? The weeklies individually come out once every seven days, the evening comes out four times a day over six days. There could well be a gap of six days between the time you send your article to a weekly and the time it might be expected to be picked up by the evening. That may be six (or five, or four, three, two) days too late for your purposes. Today's news is tomorrow's fish wrapper, as they say in the trade.

Here's something else to ponder concerning the evening: it covers a far wider geographical area than the weeklies (there are in fact other weeklies in other districts within its circulation area). Thus, if you are, for example, planning a press release promoting an event which you believe will have wider geographical appeal than the circulation area of your local weeklies, a mention in the daily (even if simply a 'What's On?' listing) will be pretty valuable. There's certainly no excuse here for letting it go to the weeklies and sitting back and waiting for it to filter through to the evening.

The same holds true for the local commercial and BBC radio stations – both good showcases for upcoming events, especially 'drivetime' bulletins when people are commuting to, and more especially from, work and beginning to think about what they will do that evening, or over the weekend. But the two stations are different – for a biggish event, for example, the commercial station might expect you to advertise instead of putting a news release to air – it is after all in the business of making money.

Once again, too, the food chain is in operation, with the stations monitoring both weeklies and the evening paper for anything they might pick up in the way of news in addition to their own news-gathering efforts. But don't assume whatever you do that your item will automatically be picked up if you have only sent it to those at the bottom of the chain.

Now the regional daily (morning paper) – often bought by people in preference to a national daily, it tries to carry a reasonable amount of national domestic and foreign news. But are things going on at regional level which will not already be covered at a district level? Very little. Instead, the regional is able to choose the best of district news items from a much wider area, and it does its best to make sure most of the locations in its circulation area get some sort of a mention. That's how the food chain goes up – but it doesn't necessarily go in the opposite direction, down. A splash at regional level in the morning may only be worth a few lines to the evening because it is now second hand, and it might not even be considered by the weeklies especially if it falls badly in deadline terms – either too late to do much about it, or so early that it will be dead and cold by the time it is printed.

Regional television works at this same level. Its demands, commercial or BBC, are much the same as for local radio, but unless the news is 'big' it stands less chance of inclusion in bulletins or news roundups at this level.

The final mass-appeal media section includes national newspapers (serious and red-top), and national commercial and BBC radio and television. The BBC has its own network of newsrooms of course but the others have stringers and freelancers judiciously dotted around the country and on the alert for good yarns. By now the way the food chain works should be fairly obvious to you so I will not labour the point other than to say if you expect your release to be noticed at this level its contents will have to be pretty big news. But if it is, then the whole country is at your feet!

Sometimes it is possible to watch the chain in operation all the way up, from a breaking story in one of the weeklies all the way to big headlines in a national or a large item on national TV.

How you tap into all this depends on the range and nature of coverage you want and the strength of the material you have to offer. But there is plenty to consider, you'll agree.

One final area I have left to last is magazines. Time and again press officers forget entirely that there are any magazines at all, let alone magazines that are of direct interest to their sphere of operations. Take a good press directory out of the library and run your eye over those dealing with your 'subject' and the chances are there will be too many to even think about listing them! However, don't you think you should? Most are very grateful for contributions. And then there are more general magazines who might be interested in what you do and what you have to say...

Exclusives and tailoring

Should you find yourself with an item that is absolutely 'right' for a particular publication, or an item that will give you the most advantages if it appears in just the one publication, you might consider offering it on an exclusive basis, or agree to hold off sending it elsewhere until it has appeared where you want it. Of course, you run a risk here of alienating other media 'customers' you might need at some other time but now and then it does no harm, especially if you spread such favours around a bit.

I know I have said elsewhere that no editor will guarantee absolutely that any contribution will make the edition, news being such a volatile commodity, but there is a high level of honour in a commitment to use an exclusive item. Provided it's a good enough yarn it is in the right circumstances worth a shot.

Tailoring is another matter and it is one of those absolutely priceless tricks of the trade that are often overlooked. On a simple 'if it fits, wear it' level 'tailoring' means studying your target and sending them your material in a similar format to the items you see in their pages – if they go in for a few paragraphs and a picture, send a couple of paragraphs and a picture. But in its more complex form it is a very powerful tool indeed. Here, instead of putting everyone on your 'round robin' list and sending each exactly the same release (and picture if applicable), you take the trouble to write each release individually, tweaking your words and if you can your angle slightly in each case, and you make sure that of the pictures you send out, no two are exactly the same. To work effectively it is essential that the recipient knows what you are doing, e.g. you ring and say 'You've got a slightly different story from everyone else, and the best picture to go with it – nobody else has got that shot.'

If you make a habit of tailoring you will gain recognition as somebody whose work can reliably be used without much further treatment, such as a rewrite, or without the target having to send their own photographer to get a different shot from everyone else. And if it also arrives with the right target and at the right time, that's true professionalism – and your scrapbook or notice board will be full of cuttings that reflect your successes.

Tailoring in fact offers a real chance for larger national and international companies to make inroads into the lower levels of the regional press where it is traditionally assumed they cannot penetrate. What you need is a localising factor – a person or thing with associations tied to the area you want to target. Finding such a link can take a bit of research but it often pays off. Look for example to members of your workforce who have undergone promotion – where are their home towns? That's fodder for the local press where mum may still live, and so would be the fact that you sourced product material or supplies from a particular area. Taking another approach and using a customer tickbox questionnaire with perhaps an associated mass prize draw will set you up with case histories to place your company names or products in the press in the prizewinners' home area. Put a little thought into the matter and you could be pleasantly surprised by the result. Most papers I work for regularly get calls from big firms and PR companies asking hopefully if any of the material they have sent out about new products or services has been used. A plaintive little cry of despair usually greets the news that they have been discarded because there is no local content or connection. Don't put up with this and just walk away – work on it, find those connections, make it a challenge!

Holiday 'happies' and the silly season

There are particular times in the year when all the media, right across the slate, are either desperate for any stories or would like to receive stories of a particular kind – happy ones.

First the desperation – it's called the silly season, but there are two of them, one long one in the summer and a briefer one around Christmas time. Roughly they correspond to the times our MPs have left parliament and the country to look after themselves while they take their buckets and spades to the seaside, or in the case of Christmas run off to warmer climes with their press attendants. The country does not immediately plunge into chaos but nothing much happens – nobody's stirring things up for a start. The chattering classes have nothing to chatter about.

The MPs can't stay away for too long or people would start wondering why we bother with politicians at all when things seem to run on sweetly without them. But the silly seasons do tend to create big holes for a sustained period in the press and everyone is on the lookout for anything that might fill a gap or two. The astute press officer has material on hand for just this occasion – a steady supply of reasonable stories which, while they may not set the earth on fire, will at least help to idle away a few minutes of time for a reader, viewer or listener.

Now for the 'Holiday Happies'. Happy stories are usually welcome all year round but you stand a particularly good chance of getting them accepted during public bank holidays. Very conscious that they are purveying for the most part doom and gloom in the general run of things, many an editor likes to give readers the happy glow of good news to take away with them for a long weekend. Again, it is a good idea to have something prepared or brewing for just these occasions.

The tasty temptation...

A few weeks back I was lucky to turn on the television just as a programme about the life of a mayfly was being shown. This featured a fly fisherman who did his best to describe in enthusiastic terms what was going on in a trout's mind as it pondered whether or not to take his artificial fly which was, to all intents and purposes, a bunch of feathers instead of a plump snack floating downriver. Catching the fish was all about timing, art and presentation.

'Look at that,' the naturally wary trout was saying to himself. 'I want that … but wait, it could be a trap, couldn't it? But, but … but it'll soon be out of reach and dash it all, I'm going to grab it anyway!'

The trout in the fisherman's basket could be an editor who's taken what you are offering, so long as you've got it right...

That offering may have commercial undertones, even a hint of advertising, but a lot of the necessary attractive elements are all in place – the right links connecting it to the journal's readers, a clean and uncluttered presentation, attention to detail...

Gulp!

18

THE EMPOWERMENT THING

So there it is. But don't put this book down without first flexing your muscles and realising perhaps for the first time that (even if you have been co-opted into the job as a barely necessary afterthought) you have a rightful place within your organisation, not to say a very important and influential one despite the fact that this is often not generally recognised. In the outside world, too, you have considerable influence, which is more than most people within any organisation can say. Remember the media needs you and what you have to say as much as you need them. Use your powers and skills for those you represent, and for those you represent them to, with fairness and wisdom – these should always be your guiding lights – and you will go far. And an occasional touch of ruthless professionalism does not come amiss!

For the most part this is an entertaining and engaging job with many facets, and it can be highly enjoyable too. Hopefully the book has encouraged you and helped you on your way, and will lead you to greater and greater success, wherein you will gain much satisfaction.

There are many organisations catering for press and PR officers, some offering professional support and advice and often job advertisements too – rather than offering you pages of contact addresses, some of which will assuredly fall out of date, I suggest you Google 'PR Associations' on your computer and watch the list pop up. The last time I did this there were 17.5 million entries for the subject! Now, if each of them bought just one of these books…